The Administration
Of Indian Foreign Policy
Through the
United Nations

The Administration of Indian Foreign Policy Through the United Nations

By
CHARLES P. SCHLEICHER
and
J. S. BAINS

Edited by
Robert W. Gregg

1969
Oceana Publications, Inc.
Dobbs Ferry, New York

The Maxwell School Series on the Administration of Foreign Policy Through the United Nations

Editor

ROBERT W. GREGG

1. *The United Kingdom* by Rosalyn Higgins

2. *The United States* by Donald G. Bishop
   (out of print)

3. *India* by Charles P. Schleicher & J. S. Bains

Table of Contents

Preface

This work on the administration of Indian foreign policy through the United Nations is the third in the series of country studies on the subject published under the auspices of the Maxwell School of Syracuse University. It differs principally from the others by including a description of the UN System agencies operating within the country. The core of this, however, as of the other works, is an account of the administrative organization and procedures for developing and administrating policy *vis a vis* the United Nations System.

Yet it is more than this. It is impossible, or undesirable in any case, to confine one's attention to the very few organs whose sole concern is with the UN System because for the most part the UN related tasks are performed by bodies responsible for both domestic and foreign aspects of national problems. We have, therefore, while emphasizing the Indian administrative arrangements for dealing with UN matters, done so in a general context of the Indian political system.

Although we have relied on printed material, both in scholarly works and in official publications, most of our information was necessarily obtained through interviews with busy officials. We are extremely grateful for the many hours that dozens of persons in several different offices, both UN and those of the Indian Government in New Delhi, and in the Indian Permanent Mission in

New York, graciously spent in interviews with the authors. Among the many to whom we are indebted we can mention only a few. To V. M. M. Nair, then Joint Secretary in charge of the UN and Conference and Disarmament Division of the Ministry of Foreign Affairs, to J. S. Teja, First Secretary in the Indian Permanent Mission to the United Nations in New York, and to Dr. John McDiarmid, Resident Representative of the UN in India, we owe special thanks, both for giving us a great deal of information and for expediting our work in general. The senior author is grateful for a Fulbright-Hayes Grant that enabled him to spend the academic year 1966-67 in New Delhi. The Graduate School of the University of Oregon also expedited the work by a research grant.

Administration organization does not stand still; some of our facts, therefore may be outdated by the time this book is printed. We may also have erred at times in our understanding of the facts gained through interviews. We are confident, however, that our account is fairly accurate and comprehensive. For errors we alone are responsible.

CHARLES P. SCHLEICHER
Eugene, Oregon, U.S.A.

J. S. BAINS
Delhi, India

September, 1968

1

India's Role in
The United Nations System

India, an original member of both the League of Nations and the United Nations, exercised very little influence on the formulation of the constitution of either. In both she achieved membership as a British dependency. Since the League Covenant was formulated and adopted when there was no expectation, at least on the part of the British Government, that India would soon become fully internally self-governing, much less independent, Indian attitudes toward the League were regarded by the British as irrelevant. India was subsequently represented in the League by appointees of the British Government, although many of these were Indians.

Although India was to become independent within two years after the UN came into official existence, that was not foreseen until after the San Francisco Conference. Winston Churchill apparently did not expect India to play an independent role in the UN. In justifying the admission of the Ukranian and Byelorussian Soviet Socialist Republics he wrote: "For us to have four or five members, six if India is included, when Russia has only

1

one is asking a great deal of an Assembly of this kind."[1] In any case, the future political leaders of India were hardly in a position to shape the Charter from their prisons in which they had been interned in 1942, to be released only in May, 1945.[2]

At the San Francisco conference the Indian delegates introduced only four proposals, in contrast to twenty-nine by those of Australia. Even the Philippine delegation introduced slightly more. One Indian proposal was that a country more than two years in arrears in payment of dues should not vote in General Assembly elections. As subsequently extended, this proposal became Article 19 of the Charter providing for the complete suspension of voting rights of Assembly members in arrears for two years or more on payment of dues. Thus in the League, and in the UN during its formative stages, except on minor matters, India's voice and votes were spoken and cast as determined by Britain rather than by India.

The situation changed abruptly with the formation of the Indian Interim Government in September, 1946. Thus almost a year before independence was to become a reality, India's representatives were for the first time the choice of Indians and they spoke and voted accordingly in the second session of the First UN General Assembly convened in New York in the fall of that year.

Although their views were seldom officially represented, the Indian elite had and expressed opinions about the League and the UN before 1946. The views of the Congress leaders, as well as those expressed in the press, are of prime significance, the former because of their subsequent political role, and the latter because they

---

[1] Winston S. Churchill, *Triumph and Tragedy* (New York: Bantam Books, 1962), p. 308.

[2] Mrs Vijayalakshmi Pandit attended the Conference, in an unofficial capacity, as a representative of the Indian National Congress.

probably represented the prevailing attitudes and opinions of most of the other educated and politically conscious
Indians. In general, the attitude in the nineteen twenties
was a mixture of skepticism and distrust of the political
activities of the League. It was seen as the instrument of
the big powers interested in maintaining the *status quo,*
especially with respect to their colonial preserves. Even
the Mandate System was regarded as "a new form of
colonialism." The major exception to this generalization
relates to the League's social and economic activities, such
as the work of the ILO, the handling of certain minority
problems, and regulation of traffic in women and children,
all of which, as limited as they were, received favorable
comment.

As the international situation deteriorated in the nineteen thirties, and Fascism grew, Indian attitudes toward
the League changed discernably. Although critical of the
existing colonial regimes, and reluctant to support them,
Germany, Italy, and Japan were regarded as greater evils.
The Congress leaders, and the views expressed in the
press, were generally in favor of League sanctions against
the aggressors, although they favored economic measures,
and were reluctant to support the use of armed force.
Since the League failed to prevent World War II or
punish aggression, the League was discredited in Indian
eyes, as elsewhere, as an effective instrument for preserv-
ing peace.

In the opening months of World War II, most of the
Congress Leaders were willing to support the wartime
United Nations, but only on conditions that the British
Government under Churchill's leadership was unwilling
to concede. Hence-forth India was an unwilling participant in the war, and certain nationalist groups were
sympathetic with Britain's enemies.

Wartime sentiment, as expressed in the Indian press,
about the possibilities of a new postwar organization was

mixed. On the whole, proposals for the organization were regarded as attempts to resurrect rather than to replace the League, as indeed they were. Reactions to the Atlantic Charter, especially Churchill's refusal to extend its promise of freedom to dependent territories, were adverse. Attitudes toward the proposed veto in the Security Council varied. Some saw it as an obstacle to the maintenance of peace, whereas others regarded it as necessary to obtain support of the great powers. The prospect that both the United States and the Soviet Union would be members was generally regarded as favorable for the effectiveness of the new organization, for they were not only the world's strongest powers, but were also then felt by influential Indians to be anti-imperialistic. Indian opinion thus "expressed both hopes and fears at the birth of the United Nations."[3]

Despite initial Indian skepticism about the UN and inability to participate in its formative stages, since 1946 India has been an active participant in most of the activities of the system. Although disappointed with certain decisions of the organization, no influential voices have called for India's withdrawal. India is a member of all the Specialized Agencies. Indians, both as official representatives and as members of international secretariats, have occupied prominent positions and have been active participants in many of the UN bodies. Unwilling to participate in enforcement actions, as in Korea, and reluctant to support measures that would enable the General Assembly to supplant, or at least in some instances to by-pass the Security Council in taking enforcement action, India has nevertheless been a champion of pacific settlement and not only a supporter but an active and

---

[3] Report of a Study Group, The Indian Council of World Affairs, *India and the United Nations* (New York: Manhattan Publishing Company, 1957). See Chapter 1, "Development of the Indian Attitude on International Organization," pp. 1-25.

important contributor to peace-keeping activities, ranging from serving as members of truce commissions to contributing armed forces in Western Asia (the so-called Middle East) and in the Congo. She also has been an active leader in the struggle to liquidate colonialism, and has vigorously championed measures against racial discrimination. As active as she has been in these areas, India has been no less concerned with UN economic and technical assistance activities, primarily as a recipient of benefits, but also as a contributor.

India's general attitude and policy toward the UN have been shaped primarily by: 1) her stance of nonalignment; 2) a desire to reduce international tensions and the dangers of armed conflict; 3) her anti-colonial and humanitarian objectives; and 4) her interest in receiving aid in the development and modernization of her society. As leaders of a nonaligned power, Indian officials have contended that they were in a position to pursue a "positive" independent foreign policy, and thus to be neutral or to take sides in disputes in the UN as the situation warranted.

This position seems to account partly for conservative attitudes toward evolution or amendment of the UN Charter that would modify or eliminate the veto on certain issues, and on enforcement measures generally as evidenced by its disapproval of the Uniting for Peace Resolution. The Indian view has been that such changes would likely lead to a break-up of the UN by causing the withdrawal of the Soviet Union and other communist countries, or would convert it into an anti-communist alliance. Either would be disastrous to the development of the organization in its role as a mediator and conciliator, as well as an effective agent in the social and economic realm.

Furthermore, in contrast to the western view that the Soviet Union used the veto only in its own narrow self interest, the Indian and many other Afro-Asian nations believed it was used in defence of their interests as well. Arthur Lall, a former permanent representative of India at the United Nations, wrote:

> While it is, of course, clear that the Soviets would not call the veto into play unless it furthered their own international position or interests, it is well to remember that the Soviet veto has not always been cast directly to safeguard a Soviet position. . . . It is well to bear in mind that this is how many Asian states have viewed the exercise of the Soviet power. In short, to them the use of the veto has been not a manifestation of a Machiavellian Soviet policy aimed at frustrating efforts to bring order into a specific dangerous situation but rather an insistence by the Soviets that the parties concerned must find the ways and means of agreeing in direct negotiations to resolve, or at any rate alleviate, the threatening situations in which they find themselves.[4]

Like most other members, however, India has taken a more "liberal" view of the Charter when it has seemed advantageous to do so. Thus she has championed attempts to "liberalize" it to enable the UN to play an active role in "non-self-governing areas," and in doing so has found herself in opposition to the colonial powers which, on matters such as this, were strict constructionists.

India's active and extensive participation in the UN system requires administrative machinery and personnel to formulate and implement policy in the system. Moreover, since the system functions within India, as well as in New York and elsewhere, Indian administrators are also concerned with activities of the UN on their own soil. Whether this comes under the rubric of *foreign* policy is irrelevant; it is a part of Indian concern with the UN system. Since this study deals with the administration rather than the substance of policy, in the following pages we shall first consider UN system operations in India and then describe and analyze the organization, procedures,

---

[4] Arthur Lall, "The United Nations and the Asian Nations," *International Organization*, XIX (Summer, 1965), 733-34.

and personnel of the Indian government for the implementation of policy in and toward that system. The
remaining sections will consider India's contributions in
personnel, finance, technical assistance and peace-keeping
activities, and formally the Indian public and the UN.

2

United Nations
Field Operations in India

India's Administration of its UN policy requires attention principally to matters before the UN organs and Specialized Agencies in New York, Geneva, Rome, and other UN "capitals." But it also calls for policy toward and relations with visiting missions as well as field offices of the system operating in India. Since the India-based UN operations are less well known than is the general system, some attention will be given to the former primarily in order to provide the local setting in which Indian administrative agencies operate. They are, however, important in their own right.[5]

The UN investment in social and economic programs in India is "by far the largest in the world."[6] This con-

---

[5] For a general treatment of UN field operations see: Walter R. Sharp, *Field Administration in the United Nations System: The Conduct of International Economic Programs.* (New York: Frederick A. Praeger, 1961); "The Administration of United Nations Operational Programs," *International Organization,* XIX (Summer 1965), 581-602.

[6] Secretary General U Thant in a statement in New Delhi, April 16, 1967.

centration reflects the fact that India has more than double the population of any UN member represented in the system, her per capita income is among the lowest of any country in the world, and her receptiveness and ability to utilize aid is relatively high.

Altogether there are nine UN and Specialized Agency offices in India. Seven of them carry on economic and social programs, one is responsible for an information program, and another is engaged in peace-keeping activities. Three of the nine offices are the regional headquarters for larger Asian areas, and another is a subregional headquarters although in all but one of these programs India has the greatest concentration of personnel and receives considerably more assistance than any other country, although not necessarily more per capita. The Asian regional offices are those of UNICEF, WHO, and UNMOGIP. The area of the first includes, in addition to India, Afghanistan, the Maldive Islands, Nepal, Ceylon and Mongolia. A considerably larger area embracing nine states in all—India, Afghanistan, Ceylon, Burma, Indonesia, the Maldive Islands, Mongolia, Nepal, and Thailand, is the concern of WHO. The peace-keeping force, the United Nations Military Observer Group in India and Pakistan (UNMOGIP), which has been in operation since 1948, alternates its headquarters between India and Pakistan, spending six months of the year in each country. Its Indian headquarters are in Srinagar, Kashmir, although a small permanent office is also maintained in New Delhi. FAO maintains in India a subregional office for the Western Zone of its Regional Office for Asia and the Far East, which is located in Bangkok. The Western Zone includes India, Ceylon and Nepal. Although the responsibility of the UNESCO office in India is confined to India, the Chief of the Mission is also Director of the South Asia Science Co-operation Office.

Five of the seven economic and social operations are conducted by Specialized Agencies—ILO, FAO, WHO, IBRD, and UNESCO. The remaining two are carried out by UN programs, UNICEF and the United Nations Development Programme (UNDP). The information program, the responsibility of the United Nations Information Service, is also a UN program. Their offices are, with the exception of UNDP and UNIS, housed in different buildings dispersed over a wide area of New Delhi. Only WHO has a modern office building. Seven of the nine offices are in converted residences and, like many residents of New Delhi, the agencies have "landlord" problems.

Officials of some, but not all, of the agencies have expressed the view that the location and facilities of the agencies were not conducive to economy, resulted in less efficiency than would centralized and better accommodations, and impeded joint coordination of policy and implementation. Indian government officials have likewise believed it would be more convenient and economical if they were able to deal with centrally located UN offices. In 1961, the Government of India promised to construct a headquarters for the UN offices which would be occupied by all of them except WHO. The conflict with China and subsequent economic difficulties interfered with these plans, although negotiations between the UN Resident Representative and the Government were still under way in 1967.

Although for the most part each of the nine field offices has a fairly well demarcated area of responsibility, their activities are in many instances closely related, and there is competition among some of them for UNDP projects. Moreover, several offices participate in joint programs. UNICEF, for example, supports a number of Government programs to which the Specialized Agencies such as FAO, ILO, and UNESCO, as well as UNDP, also contribute. Coordination among the offices is maintained by informal as well as through institutionalized channels, with the UN Resident Representative, who is also in charge of UNDP activities, serving as the principal co-ordinator, officially in some cases and by general consent in others.

UNDP and the UN Resident Representative

The Resident Representative is responsible for the administration in India of the UNDP, the World Food Program (WFP), and the UNIS. "He does, then, in fact represent the focal point of the United Nations complex for the programming, planning and co-ordination of technical assistance activities in the country."[7]

The UNDP Office evolved out of the field agency of the Technical Assistance Board (TAB), established in 1952. In 1959, following creation of the UN Special Fund, it became responsible for both EPTA and Special Fund administration. In 1967 there were seventy-six members of the UNDP staff, all but two in the New Delhi office. Ten of these were on the International Staff and the remainder were local Indian nationals. In 1966, the office budget was $214,318. Under UNDP there are two types of projects, Special Fund (SF) and Technical Assistance (TA).

Twelve of the forty-one UNDP (SF) projects, the first of which began in 1959, had been completed by 1967, leaving twenty-nine still active. The United Nations was the Executing Agency (administrator) for eight of the total and the Specialized Agencies for the remainder, the latter providing a variety of technical skills. (See Table I. below) The total project costs were approximately $150 million, with the Special Fund contributing

---

[7] Technical Assistance Board-Special Fund, Field Manual, Section II, August 1, 1965, p. 5.

about $40,202,251 and the Indian Government over $107 million.

TABLE I

Executing Agencies for UNDP—(SF) Projects (1967)

	Active	Completed
ILO	4	5
FAO	8	1
UNESCO	8	
UN	6	2
WHO	2	2
WMO		1
ICAO		1
ITU	1	
Total	29	12 (41)

Ten different Indian government organs have been involved in these projects, including those of the states. The Union Government agencies most frequently concerned were Food, Agriculture and Community Development and Cooperation (hereafter designated as Food and Agriculture) (10 projects); the Council of Scientific and Industrial Research (7); Labour, Employment and Rehabilitation (6); and Education (5). The others have been responsible for from one to three projects.

The Resident Representative has generally served as the agent of the UN for coordinating these programs. He has also been responsible for administering those of three Specialized Agencies (WMO, ICAO, ITU), each with one project, that did not have offices in India. The Resident Representative meets frequently with UN system agency representatives to discuss developments and problems of mutual interest, especially in relationship to Special Fund projects. Although the Resident Representative is not always sufficiently informed about the projects carried on by the Specialized Agencies under their "regular" programs to enable him to coordinate as effectively as may be desirable (although this is disputable and disputed), the difficulty does not usually arise when UNDP (SF) funds are involved.

The Technical Assistance Sector program of UNDP has been in some respect more extensive, but less costly, than that of the Special Fund. From 1951 to the end of 1966, UN expenditures were $38,153,000, of which $30 million was for personnel and the remainder for equipment. Some 1700 Indians were sent abroad and 1800 foreign experts brought to India. As of April 1967, fifty-three programs had been approved. The allocation of responsibility for their supervision is indicated in Table No. II.

TABLE II

Executing Agencies for UNDP (TA) Projects

UN	8
IAEA	1
ILO	4
FAO	9
UNESCO	15
WHO	12
ICAO	1
ITU	1
WMO	1
Total	53

Nineteen different Union Ministries or other organs conduct technical assistance programs in cooperation with the Executing Agencies. Three, however, have been responsible for thirty-eight of the fifty-three: Health and Family Planning (13); Food and Agriculture (12); and Education (13). Each of the other Ministries has been involved in only one or two programs. Altogether twenty-three different Government agencies, three at the State level, have been involved in administering the ninety-four UNDP projects of both Special Fund and technical assistance character. Three agencies, however, were responsible for more than half (53) of the total.

Because of the wide range of its activities in India, UNDP works with the various government agencies indicated above. However the Department of Economic Affairs of the Ministry of Finance is the channel of communication through which the Government requests assistance. On some matters UNDP also deals with the Planning Commission member responsible for UN affairs. On occasion it comes into contact with the Ministry of External Affairs. In the latter case, the Resident Representative presents his credentials to the Minister and sometimes makes courtesy calls on his office. Most of his business with the Ministry, primarily concerning protocol matters, is with the Joint Secretary who heads the UN and Conference and Disarmament and the Protocol and Consular Divisions. On occasion it has been necessary to transact business with the Foreign Secretary. UNDP's relations with State Governments have been through the Chief Ministers, or through particular Ministries, as in Madras where two large UNDP-aided projects were the responsibility of the Ministries of Public Work and Industry and of Labour and Housing.

There tends to be a "stream" of correspondence between UNDP and agency offices and the Ministries and other Government bodies, but it is usually necessary to follow this up by telephone calls and personal visits. When several Government agencies are involved in common projects, UNDP sometimes requests a joint meeting of those concerned, usually through the Planning Commission. Although not formally a member of any of the Government Consultative Agencies, which meet on an average of every six months or oftener if necessary, both UNDP and other UN offices are usually invited to attend their meetings.

Wherever the UN system operates in the field the role, or potential role, of the Resident Representative is as delicate as it is important, and sometimes as controversial. One of the principal advantages claimed for the merger of the ETAP and Special Fund, with the field activities of both under the direction of the Resident Representative, was that it would simplify contacts with governments as well as facilitate better coordination between the UN and its related agencies. Writing in 1965 of UN field operation in general, without specific reference to India, Sharp maintained that there was a "conscious effort to convert . . . [the UNDP Office] into a kind of across-the-board coordinating office, at least *de facto* (since the separate 'autonomies' of the specialized agencies must be given official recognition.)"[8]

What was said in general prior to the merger of the two programs in UNDP still holds true in India: ". . . it is very difficult to define the role of the Resident Representative/Director of Special Fund Programmes in complete and absolute terms."[9] Since 1950, when the first TAB "Liaison Officers" were appointed, the role of the Resident Representatives has undergone continuous if undramatic change. The adoption of ten "principles of Coordination" in 1961 constituted a land-mark in the development of the role of the Resident Representative, but that role is still in the process of change. The controversy that has at times characterized consideration of this issue at the headquarters level has also left its mark in the field in India as elsewhere. The scope of the responsibilities of a Resident Representative is set forth in the *Field Manual*, but its terms are very general and much is left to "responsibilities which he may be asked to perform."[10] Moreover, his responsibilities seem to be in excess of his authority and power, so that his effectiveness depends

---

[8] Sharp, "The Administration of United Nations Operational Programs," p. 594.

[9] Technical Assistance Board—Special Fund, Field Manual, Section II, August 1, 1965.

[10] *Ibid*, Section II, p. 2.

primarily on influence, especially in relation to the Specialized Agencies. Although there has been something less than unanimity among the UN field offices in India as to his appropriate role and in some instances his actual authority and functions, the Resident Representative has assumed certain responsibilities in each of the categories listed in the *Field Manual*. These are representation, information, administration, program planning and implementation, evaluation and reporting, protocol, and personal security in case of crisis.

In addition to the usual informal devices of the telephone and social occasions, coordination within the "UN family" is carried out by sending memoranda to the interested offices, through meetings of Heads of Agencies, and by distribution of the records of the proceedings. UNDP also works quite informally but effectively with the large private foundations, as well as with agencies such as USAID engaged in bilateral operations in India.

The United Nations Information Service

Although UNIS has a relatively small staff, consisting of the Director (an international staff member) and six local employees, it carries on an extensive and active program. According to the Resident Representative, UNIS is directly under his supervision. The Director, however, receives information and technical guidance from the Department of Public Information in New York, and works in India with a considerable degree of autonomy.

UNIS serves as a liaison office on a variety of matters in exchanges between UN Headquarters and Government departments, publicity media and non-governmental organizations. Film, TV, Photographic and Radio teams from Headquarters are assisted in several ways, such as working out itineraries and establishing contacts with government authorities. When conferences are held in India under UN auspices, UNIS arranges press accreditation and provides working facilities for newspaper men. UNIS Headquarters is also sent cabled summaries of press reaction and comment on the UN and matters of international importance.

The Service cooperates with the other UN system agencies, with the Indian Government, and in addition serves the Indian public directly. The Director attends meetings of the Heads of UN Agencies, and offers his services to the other field offices for publicizing their activities. UNIS, in cooperation with the office of the Resident Representative, arranges for publicizing UN activities in India. This is done primarily by providing information to newspaper correspondents, by arranging interviews with UN experts, and by taking press teams to the project sites.

UNIS works especially closely and extensively with the Ministries of Education and of Information and Broadcasting. It also maintains relations with the Ministry of External Affairs, as well as with those concerned with health, housing, food, agriculture, commerce, tourism, and planning. UNIS provides the Indian National Commission for Cooperation with UNESCO with material for distribution to educational institutions, works through the Press Information Bureau in arranging press conferences for visiting UN officials and occasionally for the circulation of background material in the form of features and press releases.

Material on the UN is translated into several local languages through arrangements made by UNIS. For example, in cooperation with the All India UN Day Committee (Ministry of External Affairs), Hindi booklets on the UN, and leaflets in twelve Indian languages are produced and distributed through the Ministry of Information and Broadcasting. All India Radio (AIR) is supplied regularly with features and weekly round-ups prepared at UN Headquarters, and documentary programs in Hindi, based on material from Headquarters, are produced under an arrangement with AIR. UNIS also works with State Directorates of Information and of Education.

In addition to assisting other UN agencies and the Government, UNIS serves the general public directly. It operates a reference library where documents and background material on the UN and the Specialized Agencies are available to educators, students, representatives of the mass media, and the general public. Press releases are made available on important issues, and special UN reports are brought to the attention of journalists specializing in economic and social affairs. Indian news agencies frequently make requests for amplification of dispatches from New York, and for background on various matters.[11]

United Nations Children's Fund

The India Office of UNICEF deals directly with all but one of the governments of the six countries under its jurisdiction. Only in Afghanistan is there a country representative. The professional staff consists of approximately thirty persons, half of whom are members of the International Staff, and the remainder of the National Professional Staff consisting of Indian nationals recruited to work only in India. Otherwise they have a similar status, except in rates of pay, leave conditions and local privileges. A small number may, however, be reclassified to the International Staff and assigned to work in other countries. It has been estimated that perhaps ninety per cent of staff time is devoted to the Indian program. A 1968 reorganization was anticipated that would lead to more country specialization and result in staff specifically responsible for operations in India.

---

[11] For a fuller description of the UN information and education program in India, see below, pp. 97-100.

In the New Delhi Office, UNICEF's relations with other offices of the UN system are intimate and extensive. It works closely with UNDP, and maintains contacts with other UN agencies, bringing to their attention matters of particular concern to mothers and children. Its work also brings it into contact with several bilateral operations. UNICEF national committees in Europe, Australia and New Zealand make special contributions to India, which the office administers, but it endeavors to keep these identifiable as "special," i.e., additional, contributions.

Its official channel of communication and liaison with the Indian Government is the Department of Social Welfare. In practice it also deals with agencies in several other ministries. Relations with the UN and Conference and Disarmament Division of the Ministry of External Affairs have ordinarily been limited to matters of general policy, terms affecting the Office itself, representation at meetings, etc. Other agencies with which UNICEF is concerned are Health, Family Planning and Community Development; Food and Agriculture; Education; Finance; the Planning Commission and various Institutes. UNICEF participates in a Government Committee responsible for coordinating the Applied Nutrition Programme. In addition to those of UNICEF, the Committee consisted of representatives of FAO, WHO, and the Ministries of Food and Agriculture, Education, and Health and Family Planning.

Under the general policy agreed to at the Centre, it has been necessary to work out operating schemes with the States. Thus UNICEF maintains relations with appropriate ministries in all the State capitals. This phase of the work, carried on primarily by Field Representatives, is extremely time-consuming. Problems arising from this aspect of UNICEF's operations varied more from Ministry to Ministry within each State than they did from state to state, depending primarily on local organization and personnel, as well as state priority given to different programs.

United Nations Educational, Scientific and Cultural Organization

The New Delhi Office staff of UNESCO consists of ten people, of whom only three or four are concerned directly with general policy matters. The principal operational activities are carried on by approximately one hundred experts working in almost every area of general UNESCO concern. UNESCO also serves as Executing Agency for eight UNDP (SF) and fifteen UNDP (TA) financed projects. In addition, it cooperates in joint UNESCO-UNICEF programs. Relations with UNDP have been quite similar to those of the other offices, especially those of the other Specialized Agencies.

Formal relations with the Indian Government are through the Ministry of Education, principally with the Secretary, who in the Indian system is the head of the permanent bureaucracy of a Ministry or in some instances of a Department. Less formal relations are maintained at lower levels with such units as the Bureau of School Education, and autonomous bodies such as the National Council for Educational Research and Training (NCERT), the University Grants Commission (UGC), and the Education Commission.

Representatives of the UNESCO Office meet frequently with the Secretary, as well as the Member-Secretary of the Education Commission. Informal telephone calls, and correspondence between the Office and the government agencies is frequent. UNESCO's representatives have often been invited to attend meetings of government officials on education matters. The Office is also usually represented at meetings of NCERT. Relations with the Ministry of External Affairs have been limited to matters such as protocol and those relating to the holding of UNESCO-sponsored conferences in India.

The UNESCO Office often signs agreements on behalf of the parent organization. For example, in April 1967, a five-year operational plan of a joint project for reorganizing and expanding science teaching in Indian schools was signed in New Delhi with a $182,000 commitment from the UNICEF for the first two years. The plan was signed by the Secretary, Ministry of Education, the Deputy Director of the UNESCO Office, and a representative of the New Delhi UNICEF Office.

The UNESCO Office arranges the itineraries of visiting UNESCO missions in consultation with the Ministries of Education and External Affairs. It also prepares the ground-work for discussion for the mission. In November 1967, a five-member UNESCO mission to study the possibility of launching a pilot project on the use of satellite communication for economic development and education had discussions with the Ministry of Education. Necessary spadework had already been done by the local Office.

International Labour Organization

The India Branch of ILO, established in 1928, has had a longer history than that of any of the other agencies. Its staff is small, consisting of the Director, a professional staff of four and approximately fourteen others. Like the other Branch Offices of ILO, the staff is local, although there appears to be a move to give it International Status. In January 1967, there were twenty ILO experts and consultants in different fields of specialization assigned to India. Out of the nine UNDP (SF) projects for which ILO had been appointed as the Executing Agency, four were still in operation, the rest having been completed. In addition, four UNDP (TA) projects were entrusted to ILO's supervision.

The main work of the Branch Office is to maintain liaison between ILO (Geneva) and India, to keep the former posted on Indian socio-economic trends, to disseminate ILO information to the Government, employers and workers and other interested parties, and to publicize its work. The Office assists, on matters within its competence, in assessing India's technical assistance requirements, and negotiates on program proposals for ILO's regular programs as well as for UNDP projects. The Branch Office also sells ILO Publications to universities, employer's and worker's organizations, and general distributors. The Government receives these free of charge. In addition, it provides supporting services to the projects, assisting the experts in various ways—as in obtaining visas, clearance of personal effects through customs, travel arrangements, establishment of initial contacts on arrival in the country, and clearance of equipment supplied as part of technical assistance programmes.

The Ministry of Labour, Employment and Rehabilitation is naturally the main government agency through which ILO works; the relationship is usually conducted formally at the Secretary level, but ILO is involved in quite extensive relations with the divisions, especially the Directorate General of Employment and Training and the Directorate General of Factory Advice. Depending on the subject matter, negotiations may also be carried on directly with other interested Departments, such as the Department of Cooperation of the Ministry of Food and Agriculture, the Ministry of Education, etc. Protocol matters are again handled through the Ministry of External Affairs.

The Director is a participating member of the Heads of UN Agencies. He collaborates with the Resident Representative on UNDP projects, both at the initial drafting stage and subsequently. He may also work with other agencies, such as UNESCO, on joint programs.

Food and Agriculture Organization

The New Delhi FAO office, responsible for the Western Zone of the Asia and the Far East Region (India, Nepal and Ceylon), devotes an estimated ninety per cent or more of its attention to India. The office based staff, headed by the Deputy Regional Representative, consisted in 1967 of a total of thirty-four persons. Of these, three were members of the International Staff and the other thirty-one Indian nationals. Although their number changes frequently, in 1967 there were forty-three FAO International personnel working on technical assistance projects in India.

FAO works jointly with several UN Agencies, especially with UNDP and UNICEF, but on some matters with WHO, ILO and others. As noted above, FAO and UNDP are jointly responsible for the WFP, with FAO giving technical guidance and advice and identifying possible projects. FAO and UNICEF participate in India's Applied Nutrition Program toward which UNICEF has contributed about one-third of the cost, partly from Freedom From Hunger Campaign (FFHC) funds collected in the United Kingdom. These two offices also participate in the Government of India's milk conservation program, the UNICEF contribution again partly financed with help from FFHC funds. In addition, FAO is the Executing Agency for eight UNDP (SF) and nine UNDP (TA) projects

On all these matters, FAO works with the Centre and State Governments in formulating proposals and implementing cooperative programs. Most of these relations are with the Ministries of Food and Agriculture, Irrigation and Power, Health and Family Planning, Education, and the Planning Commission. It also negotiates for FAO (Rome) with the Indian Government on major projects. In most cases these agreements are subject to approval in Rome but are signed in New Delhi by the Deputy Regional Representative. FAO (Rome) communicates with the Indian Government through the local office.

One of the time-consuming responsibilities of FAO's New Delhi office is the handling of fellowships, both for Indians who wish to study and work abroad and for foreigners coming to India. During the two-year period of 1965-66, approximately 175 fellowships were granted for study in India and a smaller number of Indians, approximately 109, were granted fellowships. This necessitated voluminous correspondence between FAO (India), FAO (Rome), and the Ministry of Food and Agriculture.

Since agriculture is a State subject in the Indian federal system, FAO deals with state Ministries of Agriculture as well as with the Union Ministry of Food and Agriculture. At the State level, its experience is very similar to that of UNICEF. Negotiations are conducted with the agreement of and assistance from the Centre. In all such operations, policy has been agreed to between FAO and the Centre.

World Health Organization

The WHO Regional Office for South East Asia is responsible for the UN health program in nine Asian countries. Housed in a modern office building leased from the Indian Government at a nominal rent, it is the only New Delhi UN based office with both truly functional and well-located quarters. The Regional Director, an Indian, has headed the Office during the entire nineteen years of its existence.

Of four hundred and sixty authorized posts as of June 1966, three hundred and forty-two were filled. Most of the vacancies were in the professional category. Regional headquarters personnel, excluding caretakers, cleaners, drivers, etc., consisted of one hundred and seventy-two persons, of whom eighteen were in the seven country offices of the WHO Representatives. Approximately one-third of the time of this staff was devoted to the Indian program. Of the two hundred and thirty-six authorized professional posts in the field, sixty-one were allocated to India, or about one-fourth of the professional field staff.

Of its total budget of $6.3 million (1966), approximately two-thirds consisted of regular WHO program funds and the remainder of special funds contributed through UNDP. WHO also provided technical guidance for UNICEF projects costing $5.4 million in 1966. The regular funds of WHO were allocated on a project rather than on a country basis. Approximately one-third of the total budget was for the Indian Program. Out of two hundred and two WHO-assisted projects, fifty-six were in India. There were twenty inter-country projects, some of which also benefited India.

The extent of the cooperative nature of the WHO program is indicated by the various sources of its finance. Of the total of fifty-two projects in India (1967), twenty-nine were financed by WHO alone from its regular budget (along with the Indian Government, of course), twelve were administered by WHO with UNDP (TA) assistance and two with UNDP (SF) assistance, and two employed both regular program and UNDP (SF) funds. In addition, WHO administered five projects financed from regular funds and two with UNDP Technical Assistance funds to which UNICEF gave substantial assistance. There was one UNICEF supply project to which WHO gave technical approval or advice, but no special personnel, in the community development area where the UNICEF allocation amounted to $1.3 million.[12]

Along with other UN agencies in India, WHO participates in the Heads of Agencies meetings. It also works

---

[12] See *Eighteenth Annual Report of the Regional Director, World Health Organization, Regional Office for South East Asia, August 1965—August 1966* (n.d. or place of publication given,) pp. 111-88.

closely with several UN offices on program matters. It participated in the Co-ordinating Health Programme Committee set up in India in 1965, and assigned WHO staff to assist in two projects financed by UNDP (SF) for which FAO and ECAFE were the Executing Agencies. It has advised UNDP on the health aspects of a number of UNDP (SF) financed programs. There has been especially close cooperation between UNICEF and WHO both through formal meetings and informal discussions. WHO has participated in joint negotiations with the Government on WHO-UNICEF assisted program. It has collaborated with UNICEF and FAO on the Applied Nutrition Programme, with ILO on meetings called in New Delhi to consider labor matters, with UNESCO on health aspects of general education, with IBRD on water supply problems, with USAID on malaria eradication, as well as with other bilateral programs such as the Indo-Norwegian health project in Kerala and the WHO-Danish Children's Fund in Leprosy in Andhra Pradesh. In fact, WHO has been involved in many, perhaps most, of the UN, bilateral, and private programs operating in India, for in most of them health has been an important consideration.

Because WHO is the most decentralized of the Specialized Agencies, the Regional Director is responsible for conducting negotiations with the Indian Government, and his decisions are usually accepted in Geneva. Representatives of WHO advise the Indian Government on a wide range of health matters. Although the Ministry of Health and Family Planning is the principal agency with which WHO is concerned, it has extensive and close relations with Education, and on problems involving radiation hazards, it advises the Department of Atomic Energy. On day-to-day matters business is conducted by telephone, informal visits and through correspondence. More formal contacts at the Secretary's or Minister's level have taken the form of conferences in the Government office concerned.

International Bank for Reconstruction and Development

Set up in India in the early fifties as a one-man affair, the India IBRD staff had increased by 1967 to only four professionals—three economists and an engineer—and a small number of clerical and general service employees. The four professionals and some of the secretarial members have international status; the remainder are local Indian nationals.

IBRD (Washington) is highly centralized, with all agreements being made between Headquarters and governments or private parties. One function of the India office is to work with Headquarters Missions which make frequent visits to India in connection with previous or prospective loans. Another is to analyze and to report to Washington on the economic situation and trends in India. A considerable part of the time of the staff, and all of that of the engineer, is devoted to inspection and supervision of projects financed by the IBRD "family," both for government (Centre and State) and private projects.

Relations of the field office with the Indian Government are primarily through the Economic Affairs Division of the Ministry of Finance, Food and Agriculture, and Irrigation and Power, but occasionally with several others both at the Centre and in the States. Most of these contacts are made in connection with visiting Bank Missions or in the process of supervising the administration of loan projects.

Since the office has not been an Executing Agency for UNDP projects, and has not been engaged in joint programs with other UN agencies, its relations with them are concerned primarily with general administrative problems usually considered in meetings of Heads of Agencies.

United Nations Military Observer Group in India and Pakistan

This military observation group has been on duty since 1948. Headquarters alternate between Srinagar and Rawalpindi, dividing the year equally between the two cities. Only a small office, with a Staff Officer-in-charge, is maintained in New Delhi.

Except for meeting with the Heads of UN Agencies, where UNMOGIP is concerned with common administrative problems, it has only one connection, a service one, with the other UN Agencies. It makes telecommunication facilities available between other UN India offices and their world headquarters.

UNMOGIP operates under the terms of the Karachi Agreement of 1948. This provides that it operates in India, as well as in Pakistan, through the Army Chiefs of Staffs.

3

The Conduct of
Indian Foreign Policy-
A General View

As a "Union of States", India is united by a federal system. Although in some federal systems foreign policy poses serious legal problem, this has so far not been the case in India. The Centre is endowed with full legal authority in this field. According to the Constitution it has "power" over "all matters which bring the Union into relation with any foreign country."[13] Specifically, it is made responsible for the "United Nations Organization," as well as for participation in international conferences and implementing their decisions. The sometimes ambiguous and controversial issue of the responsibility of a central government in a federal system for matters normally left to subdivisions such as "states" is met by the provision that, notwithstanding state jurisdiction, "Parliament has power to make any law for the whole or any part of the territory of India for imple-

---

[13] Constitution of India, Article 246 (1), Seventh Schedule, 10.

menting any treaty, agreement or convention with any other country or countries or any decision made at an international conference, association or other body."[14]

Problems that might arise out of the nature of the federal system affecting Indian foreign policy, and India's relationship with the UN in particular, would therefore be political and administrative rather than legal in nature. The possibility of a Centre-State conflict sometimes arises out of a situation in which the Centre negotiates an international agreement, but entrusts its administration to the states. As was noted above, even UN agencies in India deal with state governments on certain matters. The Centre is cognizant of these political and administrative realities, and the desirability of enlisting state consent and cooperation. For example, on questions involving the ILO, state governments are consulted on the selection of delegations, formulating positions on issues, and the ratification and administration of conventions.[15]

With the Congress Party firmly entrenched at the Centre prior to 1967, as well as in all the states with some exceptions for short periods of time, no serious conflicts arose in the matter of Centre-State relations that had a bearing on India's relations with the UN. The Fourth General Elections of 1967, however, changed the political situation drastically. Although Congress was returned at the Centre with a reduced majority in the Lok Sabha (House of the People), it had a clear majority in only eight states.[16] In six of the remaining states non-Congress governments were formed without serious contention.

---

[14] *Ibid*, Article 253.

[15] See A. Appadorai, "India's Participation in International Organizations—Administrative Aspects," *India Quarterly*, XVI (July-September, 1960), 55-60.

[16] Altogether there are seventeen states in the Union, but only sixteen are considered here since in Nagaland, the smallest, the situation was quite unsettled and no state elections were held.

In two, where Congress and opposition parties were rather evenly divided, Presidential rule was temporarily installed in one (Rajasthan), after which the Congress emerged victorious, and in another (Uttar Pradesh) a Congress government soon fell and was replaced by a co-alition. Subsequent splits in the Congress in two states (Madhya Pradesh and Haryana) in which Congress originally had had a clear majority, resulted in non-Congress coalition governments. Thus by the summer of 1967, Congress controlled only seven states with about one-third of the total population of the country. Late in 1967, three Non-Congress governments fell, and the future of several others was precarious. In 1968, there were several additional changes, and mid-term elections were held in three states.

Aside from possible but rather unpredictable indirect effects of these elections on Indian foreign policy in general, if some of the new non-Congress state governments, especially those few controlled by coalitions more conservative and nationalistic than the Congress, should refuse or be reluctant to participate in UN social and economic activities conducted in India, these might be reduced somewhat, or transferred to states controlled by more favorable regimes. In view of the fact that these programs have been politically non-controversial and the needs of all states for assistance great, the possible did not appear to be probable.

Government at the Centre, as well as in the states, is parliamentary in form, with its concomitant of cabinet responsibility to the legislature. The Head of State is an indirectly elected President, to whose hands the executive authority is formally entrusted. As in other parliamentary regimes, despite some constitutional ambiguity the President has been a titular executive. The Constitution provides for a Council of Ministers, headed by the Prime Minister, collectively responsible to the Lok Sabha. In actual practice, authority is exercised by the Cabinet, formerly consisting of twelve to fifteen of a larger number of Ministers, but enlarged to nineteen after the Fourth General Elections. Subject to the requirement that laws and appropriations must have the sanction of the Union Parliament, and the provision for responsibility of the Cabinet to the Lok Sabha, the Cabinet has a relatively free hand in foreign policy.

The Parliament

Both legally and politically, the Indian Union Parliament has authority and plays a role in the area of foreign policy very similar to that of the Parliament in the United Kingdom. Thus treaties and other international agreements may be negotiated and ratified by the executive without reference to Parliament. As in the United Kingdom, although they are legally binding on the state, treaties and international agreements do not become a part of domestic law unless legislation to that effect is passed by Parliament. The situation is in this respect different from that in the United States where "self-executing treaties" are a part of the supreme law of the land, but are subject to approval by a two-thirds vote of the Senate before ratification by the President. In India, unlike the situation in the United States but like that of the United Kingdom, the executive has unfettered authority over the appointment of diplomats and other foreign representatives.

Treaty implementing laws as well as appropriations are subject to approval by both the Lok Sabha and Rajya Sabha (Council of States), but the Council of Ministers is responsible only to the former. In practice, the Rajya Sabha plays a role similar to that of the British House of Lords. So far, with the Congress Party in control of both houses, the Government has been able to secure the approval of all measures relating to the United Nations, and to foreign policy in general, that it has submitted to Parliament.

Despite the dominant position of the Cabinet, however, Parliament devotes considerable time to foreign affairs. For example, in 1961 9.7 per cent (26 hrs. and 50 mins.) of the time of the Lok Sabha and 16.6 per cent (11 hrs. and 50 mins.) of the time of the Rajya Sabha was spent in considering matters of concern to the Ministry of Foreign Affairs.[17] There are various opportunities for Parliament to consider foreign policy: the question hour, debates on the President's address, adjournment and no confidence motions, and in considering implementing legislation. The Ministers are often subject to sharp attack and penetrating questions necessitating explanation and defense of various foreign policy positions. More frequently than not, the debate is in the form of a post-mortem, but this is not always the case. For example, questions of foreign aid, India's China policy, Kashmir, Western Asia, and the international control of atomic energy have been discussed at considerable length in both houses of Parliament, and undoubtedly the Government took criticisms and suggestions into consideration in framing its policies on matters such as these. As in other countries, the Government may refuse or simply refrain from divulging information on the grounds that to do so would be contrary to the "national interest," as in the case of the Sino-Indian border dispute between 1955-59. On this issue, the Government was subsequently attacked by the Congress as well as by opposition parties which

---

[17] *Report of the Department of Parliamentary Affairs,* 1961/62, Appendix III; Lok Sabha Secretariat, Second Lok Sabha: *Activities and Achievements* (New Delhi, 1962), Statements XII and XIII, pp. 24-25. The percentage of time devoted to foreign affairs in discussing the work of the other ministries, presumably considerable, was not given. Likewise, there was no indication of the amount of time spent in discussing the UN system and its activities.

contended that information had been withheld that Parliament was entitled to have placed before it.

Although there is no standing foreign affairs committee in either house, there are a number of committees that may on occasion consider foreign policy matters. Some are informal consultative committees, including the Consultative Committee for External Affairs consisting of some sixty-five to seventy ministers, ordinary members of Parliament, and senior officials. The Prime Minister and Minister of External Affairs may address a meeting of the Committee and discuss questions raised. The Committee has no formal role or authority; it is a kind of study group, and is neither very active nor influential. The Estimates and the Public Accounts Committees incidentally consider problems relating to foreign affairs, but usually their administrative rather than their policy aspects.

Thus it is fair to conclude that the legal monopoly over foreign affairs vested in the Union Government is in practice exercised by the Cabinet and permanent officials, with only limited parliamentary control.

The Administrative Structure

The major administrative divisions are designated ministries (consisting of one or more departments), departments, and boards, commissions or institutes, etc. The latter three types are autonomous or semi-autonomous bodies, although some are at least nominally attached to a ministry or department. A subdivision of a ministry is usually called a department, or in the case of the small ones a division; their subdivisions are in turn given a variety of designations, or in some instances none at all.

The number, designation, and responsibilities of the ministries change from time to time, and it appeared probable that major changes would result from the extensive investigation and recomendations of the Administrative Reform Commission, expected to make its final report in 1968. After some minor adjustments following the Fourth General Elections of 1967, especially the shifting of certain responsibilities among ministries, there were twenty ministries, nearly all of which had some responsibilities and a few major responsibilities, for foreign policy and the UN System.[18] The ministries of prime importance for the United Nation System, and whose organization and formation as they relate to that system will be considered in some detail in the following pages, are: External Affairs, Finance, Food and Agriculture, Education, Health and Family Planning, and Labour, Employment and Rehabilitation.

The ministries are headed by Ministers, most of whom are of Cabinet rank. In addition, Ministers of State, Deputy Ministers, and Parliamentary Secretaries, all members of Parliament, are assigned to the various ministries. All except the Parliamentary Secretaries are members of the Council of Ministers. These approximately fifty positions are filled by "political" appointment, formally by the President but actually by the Prime Minister.

The bulk of the staff of the ministries and other organs consists of the "permanent bureaucracy". The top rung in the permanent administrative ladder is the Secretary, a position similar to that of Permanent Secretary in the British system. The ideal model is for each ministry to be headed by a single Secretary, a major division by a

---

[18] The Ministries were: Atomic Energy; Finance; Industrial Development and Company Affairs; External Affairs; Home Affairs; Labour, and Employment and Rehabilitation; Food, Agriculture, and Community Development and Cooperation; Planning, Petroleum and Chemicals and Social Welfare; Law; Railways; Transport and Shipping; Steel, Mines and Metals; Education; Information and Broadcasting; Commerce; Tourism and Civil Aviation; Parliamentary Affairs and Communications; Defense; and Health and Family Planning.

Deputy Secretary, and a subdivision by an Undersecretary. The ideal is seldom observed; with the expansion in size and responsibility of ministries, exceptions to this arrangement have became the rule.[19] Thus although there is one Secretary or a principal Secretary in most ministries, in many instances Secretaries, additional Secretaries, or Special Secretaries, are in charge of departments or divisions of the ministries. Next in rank are the Joint Secretaries, who may head divisions directly under the principal Secretary or serve under the other Secretaries. Finally, and in the following order of ranking, are the Deputy Secretaries, the Undersecretaries, and in practise the Section Officers.

The smaller subdivisions of a ministry are serviced by a "Section," consisting of a Section Officer, a number of assistants, clerks, etc. A single section may service a subdivision, but in some cases two divisions (as in one instance in the Ministry of External Affairs) or more draw upon a single section. A section is responsible for classifying, registering, and maintaining the "receipts" and files, and making them available to the officials on their own initiative or on request. Under the conventional procedure, universally prevalent until 1958, but subsequently abolished in some divisions of the Ministry of External Affairs, as well as in some other ministries, the section performs additional functions. The files begin their long journey up the administrative hierarchy at the section assistant level, with the assistant and Section Officer recording their notes, to be added to on their upward progress. Notes may consist of "a précis of previous papers, a statement or an analysis of the questions requiring decision and suggestion as to the course of action and

---

[19] See Asok, Chanda, *Indian Administration* (London: George Allen and Union, Ltd., 1958).

orders passed thereon."[20] At the section level, "noting" is normally confined to checking and pointing out errors of fact.

The reorganization scheme of 1958 introduced some important modifications in the conventional pattern. In the "reorganized" divisions the Sections are no longer responsible for drafting and noting; this process begins at the Under-secretary (or equivalent) level. Moreover, in these divisions papers are normally supposed to be reviewed and noted by no more than two officers below the Secretary. But there are many exceptions to the supposed norm. The theory or ideal is that an officer at any level should assume the responsibility for decisions that he is competent to make and for the procedure to stop at this level. In actual practice there is a tendency, in the case of doubt, to refer problems to a higher level, either the secretarial or the ministerial. Some officials interviewed have deplored this, but few denied that it existed.

The Indian government, like any other, is organized to deal with national problems, calling for both domestic and foreign policy decisions and implementation. Few national problems can be neatly divided into their foreign and domestic components. It follows logically and practically that most of the administrative organs will be concerned with both the domestic and foreign aspects of national problems that fall within their area of responsibility. The Ministry of Foreign Affairs, therefore, like the foreign offices of other countries, has the primary but not the exclusive responsibility for India's foreign policy and relations. What is characteristic of the United States and other countries is equally so of India: "The most striking present day feature of the United States Government for the conduct of foreign affairs is the participation in all its phases of departments and agencies other than the State

---

[20] Cabinet Secretariat, *Central Secretariat: Manual of Office Procedure* (New Delhi, 1958), p. 8.

Department."[21] Three developments account primarily for the acceleration of this development: the increase in the interdependence of national societies; the assumption by governments of responsibility for many of these newer, as well as some of the older, relationships formerly left largely to non-governmental agents; and the growing multilateral approach to international problems, especially through functional agencies, but also in the general purpose organizations such as the UN.

Just as foreign policy responsibility is distributed among a number of agencies, so is that for the UN system specifically. Although each ministry or department as a whole may be concerned with UN and other foreign policy matters, many of them have found it necessary to set up units to concentrate in this area. The UN and Conference and Disarmament Division (henceforth referred to as the UN Division) of the Ministry of External Affairs is the principal one, but the UNCTAD and ECAFE units of the Ministry of Commerce, the UN section of the ministry of Finance, and the UNESCO unit of the Ministry of Education are also prominent examples.

Having distributed authority for dealing with UN and foreign policy problems among a number of agencies, it is still necessary that those problems be viewed from different perspectives, that decisions in many instances be jointly made, and that they be consistent. In short, across-the-board consultation and coordination is required. The Committee on the Indian Foreign Service (hereafter referred to as the Indian Foreign Service Committee) pointed out the necessity for and the difficulty of proper coordination.

---

[21] *Task Force Report on Foreign Affairs, Appendix H* prepared for the Commission on Organization of the Executive Branch of the Government (Washington, D.C.: Government Printing Office), p. 56.

> With the enormous growth in governmental activity, both in range and volume, and the accompanying process of fragmentation of pre-existing functions and the addition of new ones, there has been a massive enlargement of the whole apparatus of Government, so much so that coordination has become one of the major problems of the modern Civil Servant.[22]

As in Washington, London, and elsewhere, so in New Delhi coordination is attempted through a number of formal and informal means, including that of standing inter-organizational committees. One is nevertheless struck, in studying the Indian scene, how few of the latter there are, especially at the lower levels, in comparison with their proliferation in Washington and London. Does this mean that there is less coordination at these levels, and perhaps at all levels, than in many other capitals? Or is coordination accomplished by other means? It is true that within the smaller ministries, such as External Affairs, there is considerable cross-consultation through telephone calls, informal visits, and so forth. These devices and innumerable *ad hoc* ministerial conferences may take the place of more institutionalized methods elsewhere. At one time Prime Minister Shastri called for "Committeeless Wednesdays" to reduce the time spent in committee meetings. In addition, coordination through the circulation of "files", both within and among ministries, is more pronounced than in the United States and probably than in the United Kingdom. Yet in spite of these informal coordinating procedures there does appear to be a greater tendency for decisions to be made at high levels—especially the secretarial and ministerial, and possibly at the Cabinet—than in many other countries. Because of this, it seems to be assumed that coordination can take place at these levels also, and is therefore less necessary at lower levels than it would otherwise be.

[22] *Report on the Committee on the Indian Foreign Service,* New Delhi: Ministry of External Affairs, 1966, p. 24.

These are general impressions, for which we do not have hard evidence, but most officials interviewed agreed that they corresponded with their own. Furthermore, the Indian Foreign Service Committee has held that in some areas the Ministry of External Affairs was not properly equipped, and inter-ministerial mechanisms were inadequate, to enable it to carry out its assigned coordinating responsibilities. The machinery for coordination is considered in subsequent pages.

The Cabinet, Cabinet Secretariat, and High-Level Coordinating Committees

Prior to 1967, the Cabinet usually consisted of twelve to fifteen of approximately fifty Ministers collectively constituting the Council of Ministers. After the Fourth General Elections, nineteen Ministers were of Cabinet rank, with all but one heading a ministry or department. Two Ministers, although placed in charge of ministries or departments, were not members of the Cabinet.

Subject to political responsibility and responsiveness to the Parliament, and essentially to the Lok Sabha, the Cabinet has over-all responsibility for initiating foreign policy, as well as for its implementation, including that with respect to the UN.

The Cabinet is also the highest level coordinating organ. Prior to 1967, with the Congress dominant at the Centre, and with Nehru the leader of the Congress Parliamentary Party and hence Prime Minister, as well as his own Minister of External Affairs, the foreign policy responsibility was highly centralized and concentrated. Although from 1964 to 1967 the Ministry of Foreign Affairs was headed by a full-time Cabinet minister, the change seems to have made very little difference.[23]

---

[23] In the autumn of 1967, the Prime Minister, Mrs. Indira Gandhi, took over the Ministry when M. C. Chagla resigned.

Although it appears that the most important problems are considered and decisions are made at the ministerial and cabinet levels, data are not available to enable the outsider to be certain. One does, however, get the definite impression that since 1964 the Cabinet as a whole has been more active than previously.

In 1967, thirteen Cabinet Committees were reduced to seven: External Affairs; Internal Affairs; Parliamentary Affairs; Family Planning; Food and Agriculture; Tourism and Transport; and Prices, Production and Export. The Defense Committee was discontinued and its functions given to the Internal Affairs Committee. An additional committee on administrative reforms was contemplated. Each committee consists of six or seven members, mostly Ministers of Cabinet rank, but in some instances Ministers of State, the second ranking ministerial group, were included. The External Affairs Committee was composed of the Prime Minister (chairman), the Minister of External Affairs, and four or five additional ministers including those of Defense, Finance, and Commerce.

Committees of Secretaries, composed of top ranking "officials", i.e., permanent civil servants, constitute the next committee level below that of the Cabinet Committees. In number, area of responsibility, and ministries represented they resemble but are not identical with the Cabinet Committees. The Cabinet Secretary is the chairman of all of these committees. Although the committees consist of secretaries, a Joint Secretary sometimes attends meetings, along with or in the absence of the Secretary.

Two secretarial committees, one on External Affairs, and another on Economics, have been especially concerned with foreign policy, including that relating to the UN System. Although the Ministry of External Affairs was represented on both, the Committee that reported on the Indian Foreign Service in 1966 felt that the arrangement was not fully satisfactory. It recommended that the Joint Secretary of the Economic Division of the Ministry of Foreign Affairs "should maintain close contact at the highest official level with the Economic Ministries and whenever necessary with the Committee of Economic Secretaries..."[24] Whenever a Ministry is not regularly represented on a Committee, it is usually invited to send a special representative when matters of particular concern to it are under consideration.

The Cabinet and its committees, as well as the Committees of Secretaries, are served by the Cabinet Secretariat. This Secretariat is fairly large, with functions that appear to be related only tangentially, if at all, to its central task. For example it has a Department of Statistics, and Military and Intelligence "wings". Only five or six officers, however, are responsible for providing services to the Cabinet and the Committees noted above.

The Cabinet Secretary, who heads the Cabinet Secretariat, is always a senior official, and in a sense heads the entire civil service. He has been termed the "eyes and ears" of the Government and a general "trouble shooter." He could aptly be called the "Prime Minister of the Bureaucracy." He is sometimes sent abroad to represent the Prime Minister and Cabinet, especially on secret or delicate missions. Thus in 1967 L. K. Jha, then Cabinet Secretary, along with the chairman of the Atomic Energy Commission, visited London, Moscow, and Washington to present India's view on the nuclear non-proliferation treaty.

In its role of servicing the Cabinet and the high-level committees, the Cabinet Secretariat performs several important functions. It is responsible for preparing the agenda for meetings, seeing that documents and papers pre-

---

[24] *Report of the Committee on the Indian Foreign Service,* p. 21.

sented by the different ministers and secretaries are in order, and keeping a record of proceedings. Decisions made by the various bodies are communicated to those responsible for their implementation, and the Cabinet Secretariat is responsible for "follow-up." Ministries are supposed to keep the Cabinet Secretariat generally informed about their work, and especially to report on altered circumstances that may call for changes in policy or policy implementation. The Cabinet Secretariat may also bring the attention of the proper authorities to a need for reallocation of functions among Ministries.

In addition to the Cabinet and Committees of Secretaries, there were several others involved in the conduct of foreign policy, although only occasionally or incidentally with respect to the UN. Of these, the Policy Planning and Review Committee, established in 1966, is potentially the most important. It consists of the three Secretaries of the Ministry of External Affairs, the Chairman of the Joint Intelligence Committee, and others appointed by the Foreign Minister. The Secretary of the Ministry of Commerce was thus appointed. The Joint Secretary of the newly-established Policy Planning Division (Ministry of External Affairs) is the Member-Secretary. The Indian Foreign Service Committee suggested that:

> Since the scope of review by the Committee will embrace economic, defence and other aspects of foreign policy, it will be open to the Chairman to co-opt, as and when required, the Secretaries to the Government of India in other concerned Ministries, the Chairman, Chiefs of Staff Committee and the Directors of the Intelligence Bureau and Military Intelligence.[25]

The term "potentially the most important" is applicable because the Committee began its work only in 1966. As the above Report held, "If the deliberations of the

---

[25] *Ibid,* p. 25.

Committee are to be fruitful, its members must have ready access to available information ... and be provided a thorough technical analysis of the subject from all angles." The Report saw in the Policy Planning and Review Division a "suitable machinery ... for feeding the Committee with the right and required amount of material." The Committee reports directly to the Foreign Minister.[26]

The Indian Foreign Service Committee reviewed the problem and responsibility of the Ministry of External Affairs for inter-ministerial coordination of foreign policy. It also made certain recommendations for additional coordinating machinery, although none related specifically to the UN system. It expressed the view that:

> ...distribution of responsibility for [External Affairs] implies not a division, as is sometimes erroneously thought, but a complementary sharing of responsibility. Where responsibility is thus shared, the Ministries concerned should consider themselves partners in a joint enterprise and act together in close cooperation, resisting the temptation arising from human factors for each to regard itself as master in its own field ... Clear acceptance of this basic principle in theory and practice must inform the exercise of the respective departmental responsibilities and would create the atmosphere for the establishment and effective working of machinery and procedures for inter-departmental collaboration.[27]

The Committee pointed out that under the Allocation of Business Rules the Ministry of External Affairs was assigned, without limitation or qualification, the subjects "External Affairs" and "Relations with Foreign States and Commonwealth Countries." But it also noted that other Ministers have been assigned areas of responsibility which "impinge on certain sectors of external affairs," and that "the view had been expressed to us by persons with different backgrounds that there had been some erosion of the responsibility that should properly attach

---

[26] *Ibid,* p. 26.
[27] *Ibid,* p. 21.

to the Ministry of External Affairs for diplomatic dealings on sectors other than the purely political."[28]

The Committee held that the effectiveness of the Ministry in meeting its coordinating responsibilities depended on both organizational arrangements and "skilled" personnel. The establishment of the Economic Division had been a proper move, but similar arrangements were called for in other areas unless the Allocation of Business Rules were "in practice to remain a dead letter." Cultural activities abroad, usually handled in other countries by the foreign office, but in India allocated to the Ministry of Education, were cited by the Committee as a prime example. Other agencies for which the Committee believed improved machinery within the Ministry of External Affairs should be set up to facilitate consultation and coordination were Defense, Information and Broadcasting, Civil Aviation and Atomic Energy.[29]

[28] *Ibid,* p. 19.
[29] *Ibid,* pp. 21-22.

4

The Ministry of
External Affairs

Building upon earlier foundations, after 1946 India organized, staffed and developed her foreign office to carry out an increasingly heavy work-load in the international field. The "nation explosion;" membership in the UN, thirteen Specialized Agencies and some seventy additional international organizations; and representation at special conferences on a variety of matters, have combined to tax the capacity of the staff of the Ministry of External Affairs. In 1965-66, India was represented at ninety-nine international conferences or similar meetings, and in 1966-67 at one hundred and fourteen, including those of the UN.[30] The total staff of the Ministry, which manned posts both in India and abroad, consisted of a total of almost 2700 Indian Foreign Service Officers

---

[30] *Report of the Ministry of External Affairs,* 1965-66, New Delhi: Government of India (n.d. given but published in 1966), pp. 113-17; ibid, 1966-67 (n.d. given, but published in 1967), pp. 100-07.

(A and B), plus a limited number of personnel from other services.[31]

The Ministry was established in 1947 as the Ministry of External Affairs and Commonwealth Relations; two years later the appendage "Commonwealth Relations" was dropped. Its predecessors were the former Departments of External Affairs and Commonwealth Relations, and in a sense the Department of Commerce which had controlled the High Commission in London. The main function of the latter had been India's trade with the United Kingdom. Each of these departments had evolved over the course of two-hundred years from organs set up by the East India Company.[32]

The Ministry is headed by the Minister of External Affairs, usually referred to as the Foreign Minister. Aside from a small number of "political appointees"—Ministers, Deputy Ministers, and Parliamentary Secretaries who work closely with the Foreign Minister, and a maximum twenty-five Heads of Mission—the remainder of the staff consists of civil servants, chiefly members of two branches of the Indian Foreign Service.

Three Secretaries, directly under the Foreign Minister, are in charge of the Ministry, which is organized in eighteen divisions. The divisions may be classified into

---

[31] A considerably larger number of persons were engaged in carrying on the foreign policy tasks. Aside from the military, there were those in the other Ministries who not only worked in New Delhi, but also participated in the delegations to international conferences, especially but by no means confined to those of the Specialized Agencies.

[32] For a fuller treatment of the subject, as well as the most comprehensive work on the administration of Indian Foreign Policy, see: N. Parameswaram Nair, *The Administration of Foreign Affairs in India—With Comparative Reference to Britain*, New Delhi: 1963 (Ph.D. thesis, Indian School of International Studies, Typed). Also see *Report of the Committee on the Indian Foreign Service*, p. 1, for a brief summary of the background of the Ministry.

four types: service (or administrative) (4), territorial (or geographical) (8), functional (5), and the United Nation and Conferences and Disarmament Division (1). The four service or administrative divisions are the Administrative, Protocol and Consular, Passport and Visa, and Communications and Security. Their functions are only incidentally relevant for the UN system. The eight territorial divisions are involved in UN affairs when issues of concern to their areas of responsibility are under consideration. Two of the five functional divisions—External Publicity and Legal and Treaties—have a similar role. The Economic Division, however, is more directly and continuosly involved, along with the UN Division, in UN System work. As we shall see in the subsequent discussion of the UN Division, it falls into a separate category.

Ministers and Parliamentary Secretaries

In conformity with the general pattern, the Ministry of External Affairs is headed by a politically appointed Minister, who is assisted by one or more similarly appointed Ministers of State, Deputy Ministers of State, and Parliamentary Secretaries. The pattern has varied over the years. Usually, however, there has been one Minister of state, or Deputy Minister, and one or two Parliamentary Secretaries. As of early 1967 there was only one such appointee—a Deputy Minister of State. In November of 1967, however, a Minister of State was added. Parliamentary Secretaries, who are not members of the Council of Ministers, correspond to parliamentary private secretaries in the United Kingdom. Their principal task is to assist the Foreign Secretary in his relations with Parliament.

The "permanent" Secretaries report directly to the Foreign Minister rather than to his political assistants. The latter do not appear to be assigned particular duties;

rather they assist the Minister in discharging his general responsibilities. Thus at this level there is no specialization in UN affairs.

The Secretaries

When the Ministry of External Affairs was organized in 1947, with Jawaharlal Nehru holding the portfolio of Minister of External Affairs, the head of the "permanent" bureaucracy of the Ministry was especially important. He was to be the "principal adviser to the Prime Minister ... and was expected to relieve him of much of the Departmental burden."[33] To emphasize his responsibility for executive control, in addition to the role of principal adviser, the position was designated as Secretary General. Except for a brief period in 1952, the post was in existence until after Nehru's death in 1964 and the retirement of the then incumbent. Under the Secretary General was the Foreign Secretary (Secretary of the former External Affairs Department), in charge of foreign policy as a whole, and an "additional", later the Commonwealth, Secretary, responsible for Commonwealth relations.

In 1951, a "Special" Secretary was appointed to deal with India's UN policy, which required considerable time and attention as a result of the Korean War and India's election to the Security Council. A year later, however, the post was abolished. In 1956, a "Special" Secretary was again appointed, this time to take charge of administration, especially of the newly-created IFS (B). Two years later, with the increasing burden of UN duties on the Secretary General, these were assigned to the Special Secretary. After the position of Secretary General was abolished, the organization and designations of the top bureaucracy were somewhat modified. The Ministery is now headed by the Foreign Secretary and two other

---

[33] *Report of the Committee on the Indian Foreign Service,* p. 1.

Secretaries designated Secretary EA-I and Secretary EA-II. The positions are filled by senior and experienced members of the IFS, and are the equivalent in rank to the more prestigous Heads of Mission. Except that the Foreign Secretary is generally responsible for coordinating the work of the Department, his authority is no greater than that of the other two Secretaries. The Committee which reported on the organization of the Ministry in 1966 found the arrangement unsatisfactory and recommended the re-creation of the post of Secretary General. "Clearly then, there is a need, such as has been generally accepted elsewhere, to have at the head of the Ministry one invested with overall responsibility.[34] The Cabinet, however, was reported to have rejected this recommendation. Although there are frequent shifts, at any particular time each of the Secretaries is responsible for the work of several specific divisions. As of 1967, the Joint Secretaries of the UN, Economic, and several of the territorial divisions reported to the Foreign Secretary.

The Secretaries, usually along with the Foreign Minister, customarily meet daily to deal with the work of the Ministry, and as indicated above, most of the policy questions are considered and considerable intra-ministerial coordination takes place in these conferences. The Secretaries also participate in the bi-weekly meetings of Joint Secretaries and Directors who head the eighteen divisions. At some of these meetings, the heads of divisions may bring up matters which they think need to be considered by several divisions. At other times an entire meeting may be devoted to a major current issue.

The UN and Conference and Disarmament Division

The Division (henceforth referred to as the UN Division), headed by a Joint Secretary, came into existence in

---

[34] *Ibid,* p. 23.

its present form only in 1960. Previously UN matters were handled by the Western Division, with a Director in charge. In addition to the Joint Secretary, the Division has two Deputy Secretaries, two Under Secretaries, three research officers, and the staff of two Sections—approximately fifty in all. Its work is divided somewhat informally between three sub-divisions designated UN-I, UN-2, and Disarmament.

The first two of these are concerned with the work of the UN and the Specialized Agencies, except disarmament, and with international conferences generally. The Disarmament Unit is responsible for Indian policy for the international reduction, limitation, and control of armaments, whether or not related to the work of the UN.

The staff of UN-1 consists of a Deputy Secretary, an Under Secretary, one research officer, and a Section Officer, his five assistants and clerical staff. Its area of special concern is with the "political" aspects of economic and social affairs, especially as these relate to ECOSOC. It is also involved in international conferences dealing with these matters. UN-2, with one Deputy Secretary, who also heads the Disarmament Unit, a Deputy Secretary and an Under Secretary, has a Document Unit with a librarian and an assistant, and a Section headed by the Section Officer with four assistants and two or three clerks. Officially the two Sections follow the conventional pattern, but in practice they fall into a "semi-reformed" category. Thus they do relatively little "noting". UN-2 is responsible for the "political" aspects of India's policy in the UN's principal organs, except ECOSOC. Like UN-1, it shares in the task of selecting delegations to UN and other conferences dealing with matters within its competence. The Disarmament Unit, with a Deputy Secretary as head who is also responsible for UN-2, does not have an Under Secretary. Instead it has a Senior Research

Officer and two research assistants. Moreover, it does not have a separate Section as such. Since the staff is integrated, it is referred to as a Unit, in contrast to UN-1 and UN-2 which are called Sections. The Indian Foreign Service Committee has suggested that "work connected with Disarmament may... increase sufficiently to justify, at a future date, a separate Division dealing exclusively with it."[35] In view of India's vital concern with disarmament, the nuclear non-proliferation treaty, and her membership on the eighteen-member Disarmament Committee, one can only wonder whether the need for a separate division will be greater at a "future date" than it was when those lines were written.

It was noted above that the UN Division stands in a class by itself. It is clearly distinguishable from the administrative divisions. It is also different from the territorial divisions in that its concerns are global. And unlike the functional divisions, although their duties are likewise not confined to particular geographical areas, it is concerned with all aspects of India's policy in regard to matters before the UN.

Nevertheless, it is true that the Economic Division of the Ministry of External Affairs and several other ministries are more deeply involved in economic, commercial, cultural, educational, and social aspects of India's UN policies than is the UN Division, especially as these relate to the Specialized Agencies. It is sometimes, perhaps generally, held that the particular province of the Division is "political" matters, or the political aspects of economic, cultural, and similar problems. At the same time the territorial divisions are almost equally concerned with political matters. The difficulty is that "political" does not appear to be a discreet category of human affairs distinguishable from the economic, etc. The working rule is

---

[35] *Ibid*, p. 28.

for the UN Division at least to assume the initiative on matters such as elections to UN organs, except to the Specialized Agencies, to work particularly closely with the territorial divisions on matters that are or are likely to be internationally controversial, and to take the leadership in coordinating general UN policy within the Ministry.

The work of the Division falls into four categories. The first relates to matters in which it has the primary responsibility. Disarmament is a clear example. Although almost all decisions in this vital area are taken at high levels, and policy proposals require consultation with several ministries, including Defense, the Division is responsible for the disarmament spade-work of the Ministry of External Affairs, and for implementing decisions relating thereto. It also has the primary responsibility for so-called political UN questions, such as membership in UN system organs, election of Indian and other representatives to these bodies, and many matters, especially controversial ones, which are considered in the Security Council, General Assembly, and other organs.

Practically all these matters require wide clearance within the Ministry, with one or more territorial divisions in most instances, with the Legal and Treaty Division on questions of international law or the legal aspects of prospective international agreements, and with the Economic Division if the matter is primarily economic or has economic implications. Since the Division shares responsibility in a general way for UN matters of concern to many other ministries, it is supposed to be kept informed of their work, to examine new proposals, especially to see if they correspond to general policy, and to suggest changes when it deems them advisable. At the Under Secretary and Deputy Secretary levels of the UN Division, informal consultations and the circulation of files take place with their counterparts within the Ministry and among Ministries. At the Division-Head level, matters of common concern may be considered at the biweekly meetings of Joint Secretaries, Directors and Secretaries.

Secondly, the UN Division is at least one of the clearance points on economic, social, and related issues, even though these are frequently the primary concern of other "operating" ministries. The Economic Division of the Ministry, however, is probably more active in regard to many of these economic matters than is the UN Division.

Thirdly, the Division is concerned with all UN and other international conferences in which India participates. It is kept informed of conferences in which other Ministries are the principal participants, and makes recommendations regarding the composition of delegations. The composition of most delegations, however, especially those sent to the General Assembly, is decided at high levels in the Ministry or even by the Cabinet.

Fourthly, as noted above, it has a limited role in working with the UN System field offices operating in India. This role involves such matters as general policy, representation at meetings, and arrangements for holding UN meetings in India.

Economic Division

The role of the Ministry of External Affairs in economic and commercial matters has been a somewhat controversial one. Two factors seem to have been contributed to this situation. First, other ministries, as in other countries, have been less than anxious to share their responsibilities, and second, according to the Indian Foreign Service Committee, IFS officers on the whole have been neither sufficiently expert nor even especially interested in the more specialized "non-political" areas of policy and relations. After noting that when the IFS was being established in 1947 some officers were chosen because of their commercial background and experience, the Committee wrote: "Notwithstanding this, the tendency appears to have grown over the years, to regard commercial, and latterly also economic, work as either less attractive, or too specialized and narrow in scope."[36]

The history of the Division reflects this situation. An Economic Division was established in 1947, but disbanded in 1950 as an economic measure. One of the senior officials wrote in 1956:

> The Ministry of External Affairs has no economic or legal sections of its own, and though this deficiency is to some extent made good by the frequency of inter-departmental consultations, the lack in particular of an economic section must, in my personal opinion, be regarded as an unfortunate weakness in the structure of the Ministry responsible for handling international relations in the conditions of the modern world.[37]

The unit was created in 1961 as the Economic and Coordination Division, but "Coordination" was subsequently dropped from the title. Although the Division was long regarded as "temporary," it is now apparently accepted as an essential part of the Ministry.

There is both a Joint Secretary and a Director of the Division. Although the former is the Head, general supervision and responsibility are shared by both. The Division Head reports directly to the Foreign Secretary. In addition to these two officials there are six staff members with the rank of Under Secretary, but there are no Deputy Secretaries. The entire Division is served by one Section, consisting of a Section Officer, six assistants, an accountant, and a number of clerks. The Economic Division, unlike the UN Division, is "reorganized."

---

[36] *Ibid*, p. 43.

[37] H. Dayal "The Organization of Diplomatic and Consular Services, with special reference to India," *India Quarterly* XII (July-September, 1956), 275-76, as cited in Nair, *The Administration of Foreign Affairs in India*, p. 286.

As in the UN Division, the work-load of the Economic Division is informally divided among sub-units. One of these is known as the Technical Cooperation Cell. Manned by three IFS (A) Officers, it is responsible primarily for assisting in the implementation of certain technical assistance agreements entered into by the Indian Government. For example, India has agreed to furnish experts such as doctors to several developing countries, and to provide technical training in India for personnel from these countries. The Cell works closely with the Special Committee for Assistance to African Peoples (SCAPE), for which the Department of Economics in the Ministry of Finance is primarily responsible.

The second sub-division, with one IFS (B) officer and two members of the Indian Economic Services, is more concerned with policy development than is the first. The IFS (B) officer, however, devotes his time mainly to general administrative work in the Division, to maintaining liaison with the private foundations, and to routine clearance. The other two officers have certain defined duties, but a great deal is left to their discretion. The fact that they were not selected from the IFS seems to substantiate the contention of the Indian Foreign Service Committee concerning the economic competence and interest of the Service. The two Deputy Secretaries are frequently engaged in "spade-work" such as preparing briefs and estimates of the worth and feasibility of economic cooperation with specified countries. These are then routed to other Ministries—Commerce and Finance in particular, and to the Planning Commission. The unit is also concerned with India's commercial relations generally with respect to which it provides analyses and advice and serves as a "watch-dog" in clarifying briefs prepared by other organs. This brings it into relations with other ministries concerned with transportation, civil aviation, food, agriculture, health, and education. At one time the Division was responsible for duty-free entry of relief supplies, but this wa later shifted to the Department of Social Welfare, with the Economic Division retaining only the responsibility for considering new institutions requesting the privilege. If agreement is not forthcoming at lower levels, an issue may be submitted for resolution to the Committee of Economic Secretaries. Within the Ministry, close liaison is maintained with the territorial divisions, and on appropriate matters with the UN Division. All agreements, and problems relating to the interpretation of existing agreements, are cleared with the Legal and Treaties Division. Problems may be considered at meetings of Heads of Department and Secretaries. The officers have estimated that the contacts of the Division were in the proportion of three within the Ministry to two outside.

The Division is concerned with India's UN policy and relations primarily as they relate to its general work. The agenda of ECOSOC, referred to it by the UN Division, is examined, and it is kept informed of the work of the other Ministries who have the primary responsibility for the Specialized Agencies. The Division may also participate in UN conferences that fall within its sphere of interest. The Joint Secretary, for example, was a member of the 1967 ECAFE meeting held in Tokyo, and was made responsible for approximately a fourth of the agenda. In preparing for the meeting, basic material, briefs, and recommendations from other interested ministries were given shape in the Economic Division, which was responsible for final clearance. It was particularly alert to ascertain that the treatment of an issue should be balanced and complete, and that recommendations be in conformity with general policy. In case of doubt on any of these points a brief might be referred back to a ministry with suggestions that points be made clear or amplified. Only occasionally does the Economic Division become involved in relations with the India-based UN field offices, although it has at times dealt with **UNDP** on technical assistance problems. For example, it once considered a UNDP-ECAFE proposal for a project involving the assistance of a team of French hydraulic engineers.

Other Divisions

Most of the Divisions of the Ministry are involved, directly or incidentally, in work relating to the UN. References have been made to the territorial divisions and to the Treaties and Legal Division. The External Publicity Division sometimes comes into the picture, as do the Protocol and Consular, Passports and Visa, and Communication and Security Divisions, in the performance of their regular duties. The Planning Division could be of considerable importance. Only the territorial, the External Publicity, and the Legal and Treaties divisions warrant comment here; the work of the others as they relate to the UN are either relatively unimportant or routine.

In structure and staffing, the territorial divisions conform to the usual pattern, except that they are, in some cases, headed by Directors, who are lower in rank, and usually younger and less experienced than are the Joint Secretaries of most of the other divisions. The Indian Foreign Service Committee suggested that about three-fourths of the department heads should have Joint Secretary status.[38] Most of the territorial divisions have a smaller staff than do the others. One division responsible for a large and important area has only three Deputy Secretaries and the Director. It shares the services of a Section with another division.

The territorial divisions, as previously noted, are kept informed about UN matters affecting their areas of re-

---

[38] *Report of the Committee on the Indian Foreign Service,* p. 28.

sponsibility, usually by the UN Division, but on certain matters by the Economic Division. Their views may be expressed either upon their own initiative or by request of the UN or Economic Division.

Depending on the nature of the problem, the territorial divisions frequently find it necessary to work with the other ministries. On matters such as scholarships, this is for some of them practically a daily part of their activities. They also advise the Ministries of Food and Agriculture, of Finance, and the Planning Commission on economic aid and technical assistance programs. Some, but not a substantial part, of this work is directly related to the United Nations. Officers interviewed could not recall having official dealings with the UN Field Offices in New Delhi.

Prior to 1957, when the Legal and Treaties Division was established, there was only one Legal Adviser in the Ministry of External Affairs. The Law Ministry was therefore relied upon for legal assistance and advice. The Division is headed by a Legal Adviser with the rank of Joint Secretary. Under him are ten specially recruited officers with competence in international law, none of whom is a member of the Indian Foreign Service. The Indian Foreign Service Committee has indicated that there has been some discontent among the officers over rates of pay and promotion opportunities, but it has recommended against pay parity with Foreign Service Officers.[39] The Division is subdivided into three branches specializing in general international law, private international law, and the UN and other international organizations.

The Division serves as adviser on international law to the government in general, but on UN matters it deals primarily with the UN Division. Nevertheless, it occa-

---

[39] *Ibid.,* p. 37.

sionally advises the Economic Division, and also the territorial divisions on UN legal questions. Although prepared to render advice to other ministries, it is only infrequently called upon to do so. Legal officers from the Division are sometimes regular members of delegations to UN conferences, and usually serve as advisers to such delegations.

Responsibility for external publicity was transferred from the Department of Information and Broadcasting to the Ministry of External Affairs in 1948, although the former handled all such publicity in New Delhi for the next ten years, and continues to do so for publicity within India. It also supplies most of the material for use abroad by the Ministry of External Affairs. The Division briefs the press, both Indian and foreign, operating from New Delhi, participates in policy formation and implementation, including supervision of publicity posts abroad, and supplies information and material for dissemination abroad.

The Division is headed by a Joint Secretary, who also has been responsible for Parliamentary relations. As of 1967, it appeared that his responsibilities would henceforth be restricted to external publicity. The Joint Secretary is one of the chief spokesmen for the government on foreign policy matters, and thus works closely with the other Joint Secretaries, Directors, and Secretaries.

The day-to-day-management of the Division is left to the Director of External Publicity who is responsible to the Joint Secretary. The Division is subdivided into two branches, the Information Service of India (ISI) and Public Relations. The ISI is in turn divided into three "wings"—functional, territorial, and transmission. Of approximately ten officers in New Delhi, three are Indian Foreign Service Officers, and the remainder officers specially recruited before 1959, after which the practice was stopped, on terms different from those provided by the

Indian Foreign Service. The eight Section Officers and Section employees are members of IFS (B).

As in the case of the Legal and Treaties Division, most but not all of the relations of the External Publicity Division relating to the UN are with the UN Division; it deals with other Divisions within the Ministry, and with other ministries very much as does the Legal and Treaties Division. The major exception is the special relationship with the Ministry of Information and Broadcasting noted above. Publicity about the UN, especially on problems of particular importance to India, may be initiated by either the Division of External Publicity or other divisions, especially the UN Division. In all cases there is general clearance among the parties concerned. Each of the other ministries has its own publicity apparatus, and the External Publicity Division may work with them or with other persons in giving publicity abroad to matters such as commerce, opportunities for foreign investment in India, etc. UN matters are treated as a part of general publicity. The Division sometimes consults with the Director of the UN Information Service, especially in publicizing visits of UN dignitaries.

Personnel

Most of the positions of the Ministry of External Affairs, at home and abroad, are filled by the same 2700 members of the two branches of the Indian Foreign Service. The principal exceptions are the "political" appointees, approximately thirty, and the bulk of the officers of the External Publicity and Legal and Treaties Divisions. In addition, there are a few other exceptions, such as the two members of the Indian Economic Service in the Economic Division. None of the staff is recruited or trained with a view to UN work. Whatever specialized competence may be found in that regard derives from experience. In this respect India is not different from other countries. However, since the UN system calls for the same kind of general and expert competence as does international affairs generally, specialization is hardly a practical proposition. To the extent that India's representatives may lack special competence as "diplomats in international cooperation," it is a weakness shared with those of other countries. The reservoir upon which India draws for dealing with the UN, therefore, is a common source for her general foreign service.

The recruitment, training, and experience of the vast majority of the foreign service staff has taken place over the past twenty years. In 1946, the Prime Minister stated that with a need for over three hundred persons to man posts from the top grade down to the lowest, Indian officials possessing the requisite experience numbered barely fifty.[40] One of India's many pressing "priorities" was to overcome the shortage.

The Indian Foreign Service was created by a decision of the Cabinet of the Interim Government in October, 1946. The original members of the Service—approximately 110 in all—were specially recruited from a number of sources: about thirty from the Secretary of States Services, and some eighty from military officers holding Emergency Commissions, Class I Officers from different departments, and from qualified persons in private life. Subsequently all *new* recruitment has been through an annual competitive examination common for the Indian Foreign Service (IFS-A) and the Indian Administrative Service (IAS). A small number have been transferred from other services, and in recent years promoted from the second branch of the Service, the IFS (B), and from the Information Service Division of the Ministry. As of January 1966, of a total of 271 IFS (A) officers, 162 had been recruited through the regular competitive examination

---

[40] Press conference statement, cited in Nair, *The Administration of Foreign Affairs in India,* p. 566.

procedure; the remainder represented the hold-overs from the original special recruitment and those transferred or promoted from other services.

TABLE III

IFS (A) Cadre (as of January 1966)

I. Original Special Recruitment

Permanently seconded from other services 20
Selected through the Federal Public Service Com-
    mission 33
Selected through the Special Selection Board 33

II. Promotion

From Information Service Posts 5
From the IFS (B) 18

III. Regular Recruitment

Through Competitive Examination 162
                                                                                    ———
    Total 271

*Source: *Report of the Committee on the Indian Foreign Service*, p. 4.

Since "seniority" plays such an important role in the Indian promotion scheme, most of the top positions in the service are filled by those specially recruited in the early years. In the near future the situation will change as men grow older and move upward on the promotion ladder. There is some indication of resentment with what is referred to as "ICS [recruits from the civil service of British days] domination," a situation reminiscent of the feeling among the Foreign Service Officers and those of the Department of State before the "integration" of the American Foreign Service.

Recruitment, the selection process, training, career specialization, pay and allowances, and the like, present problems and provoke criticisms similar to those common to the foreign service of other countries. In India, as in other underdeveloped countries, some of the conditions are more severe than in affluent societies.

The bulk of the members of the Indian Foreign Service are in the IFS (B) branch.[41] Organized only in 1956, it is a kind of "junior" service, with its members subject to assignment at home and abroad. For the most part the Sections are staffed with IFS (B) personnel, although a few fill higher positions, but not very high ones, not normally filled by Foreign Service Officers. In 1967, there were approximately 2500 members of IFS (B), some 1960 in permanent and the remainder in temporary posts.[42]

The branch is divided into three Cadres or Sub-Cadres, as follows: General Cadre (Grades I-VI (Grades II and III are integrated); Stenographer Sub-Cadre (Grades I and II); and Cypher-Sub-Cadre (Grades I and II). Grade I officers, all of whom are promoted from Grades II-III rather than directly recruited, serve as Under Secretaries at home and as Second Secretaries abroad. After six years of service they are eligible for promotion to the rank of First Secretary. Of the other Cadres and Grades, some are selected through promotion and others by recruitment. The Indian Foreign Service Commission noted the "bottom heavy" strength of the Indian Foreign Service as a whole, and especially of the IFS (B). It recommended a reform in this particular, one which it believed would, along with some related changes, result in better use of manpower at no increase in monetary outlay.[43]

---

[41] The usual practice in India is to refer to the IFS (A) as the Indian Foreign Service, and its second branch as IFS (B).

[42] *Ibid,* p. 105.

[43] *Ibid,* pp. 107-8.

5

Other Ministries and Organs

Six ministries and their closely related organs, in addition to the Ministry of External Affairs, have been singled out for special treatment because they appear to be more intensely and extensively involved in foreign policy and UN System activities than do others. The Department of Finance is a key agency not only because of the substantive issues for which it has primary responsibility, but also because of its coordinating role. Although the Ministries of Commerce, Food and Agriculture, Education, Health and Family Planning, and Labour, Employment and Rehabilitation have some coordinating role, their primary task is policy development and implementation in their respective areas of primary concern.

Ministry of Finance

The Ministry of Finance is second to none in importance among the Union Ministries. It is responsible for managing the finances of the Union Government and for financial matters affecting the entire country. It is a key agency in the administration of Indian Policy with respect to the UN System, directly for several Specialized Agencies and their related organizations, and indirectly through its control over the budgets of other governmental organs.

India's relations with the IMF, IBRD, IDA, and IFC, as well as those with the newly established Asian Development Bank, are the direct responsibility of the Ministry. Because of the precarious economic condition of the country, especially the stringent foreign exchange situation, it holds a tight rein over the allotment of finances to the other ministries and thus ultimately affects their participation in UN activities. Though these ministries make the final decisions regarding the allocation of money for their UN work, the Ministry of Finance has a major voice in this sphere also because it is ultimately responsible for raising funds and, in cooperation with the other ministries, controls the entire expenditure of the Government of India.

The United Nations work of the Ministry is entrusted primarily to the External Finance and Foreign Aid Division of the Department of Economic Affairs, one of its three departments.[44] The Division is concerned with all matters relating to foreign exchange, including exchange control, foreign investments, and economic, financial, and technical assistance received by India or rendered by her to foreign countries. All proposals regarding trade and payment agreements with foreign countries as well as broader questions in this sphere are examined by the Division.

The External Finance and Foreign Aid Division, like other divisions of the Department, is headed by a Joint Secretary, assisted by a number of Deputy Secretaries in

---

[44] Previously the Ministry had four departments. In 1967 it was reorganized into three: Department of Expenditure, Department of Economic Affairs, and Department of Revenue and Insurance.

charge of various sections. Because of the significance of its work, the IMF and IBRD Section is headed by a Joint Secretary who is assisted by full-time Deputy Secretaries for each of the five UN monetary and fiscal organs. A sub-section, known as UN Ward, dealing with assistance, is headed by an Under Secretary and falls within the jurisdiction of the IMF and IBRD Section. Within the Division, work is coordinated by the Joint Secretary.

Some work relating to the UN is also performed by the Economic Division of the Department of Finance, but its functions are purely of an advisory character. The briefing unit of this Division prepares briefs and submits materials on financial and economic questions in connection with India's participation in the UN, its Economic and Social Council, ECAFE. UNCTAD, and other international conferences. Similarly, the international economic unit of this division reviews trends in Indian foreign trade, balance of payments, foreign aid, foreign exchange resources, and economic developments in other countries. It has also participated in the preparation of materials for the meetings of the Aid India Consortium sponsored by IBRD. The division is in charge of an Economic Adviser, assisted by a Deputy Economic Adviser, and a few Assistant Economic Advisers and Research Officers. India is also a permanent member of the UN Commission on Narcotic Drugs, and the Department of Revenue and Insurance handles work in this sphere through the Narcotic Commissioner who controls the enforcement of the international conventions.

All negotiations with IBRD and its subsidiaries are conducted through the IMF and IBRD Section of the External Finance and Foreign Aid Division, although a loan may be used to finance projects entrusted to other ministries. Ordinarily a proposal is developed by a particular ministry and then examined by the Ministry of Finance. The Ministry also studies proposals for IBRD loans to private companies because all such loans are guaranteed by the Government as is required by the bank. A financial adviser is attached to each ministry to facilitate coordination with the Ministry of Finance.

Delegations to important international conferences on financial matters are ordinarily headed by the Minister of Finance. High officials from the Department of Economic Affairs, the Governor of the Reserve Bank, representatives of other ministries in cases where matters of interest to them are considered, as well as state ministers of finance, are usually included in the delegations. Since India is a member of Board of Governors of IMF, IBRD, IDA and IFC, the Minister of Finance, or his nominee, attends their meetings. A high official of the Department of Economic Affairs, however, is posted at IBRD headquarters in Washington, D.C., to attend meetings of the various committees of which India is a member. A team of officers may also be sent from the Ministry of Finance to attend special meetings. For example, the head of the External Finance and Foreign Aid Division attended a meeting of the United Nations Development Programme in New York in 1967, and also negotiated with the US Export-Import Bank for a $4 million loan for Indian firms. Mr. C.S. Swaminathan, in charge of the IMF and IBRD Section, also attended a meeting of the Governors of IBRD on behalf of the Minister of Finance. Indian representatives have also served as Directors of these agencies. After the establishment of the Asian Development Bank, Mr. P. V. Rao was appointed as one of its regional directors, and Mr. C. S. Krishna Moorthi became the First Vice-President of the Board of Directors. India's interest in the work of these UN agencies is indicated by substantial subscriptions to their funds. With a share capital of $93 million, India is second only to Japan, which contributed $200 million, among the regional shareholders of the Asian Development Bank.[45] Similarly, after the United States, the United Kingdom, France, and Germany, India is the largest subscriber to the funds of the IMF, IBRD, IDA and IFC.[46]

Ministry of Commerce

India is one of the original twenty-three members of GATT and has continuously taken a keen interest in problems of trade and tariffs. Because she was dissatisfied with the achievements of GATT, she took a leading part in the establishment of UNCTAD. As a leader of the Afro-Asian states, she played a dominant part in the formulation of the Algiers Charter of "77." It is in this spirit that she invited the Second UNCTAD Conference to meet in New Delhi in early 1968 in order that a determined bid might be made to commit the developed nations to a more liberal policy in regard to both trade and aid.

The Ministry of Commerce has the principal responsibility for GATT and UNCTAD, as well as for trade in general, although a number of other ministries such as Finance, Industry, Food and Agriculture, and Transport and Shipping share in the work. Originally a department of the Ministry of Commerce and Industry, a separate Ministry of Commerce was created after the Fourth General Election of 1947 to give greater attention to India's trade.

---

[45] *Report 1966-67, Ministry of Finance,* New Delhi: Government of India, 1967, p. 48.

[46] For the World Bank, India contributes 3.77% of the total; for IMF, 3.7%; for IDA, 4.05% and IFC, 4.48%. India has borrowed extensively from these agencies: from the IBRD (up to March 31, 1966) $971.9 millions, from IDA $585.0 million. *External Assistance* 1965-66, New Delhi: Department of Economics Affairs, Ministry of Finance, 1966, pp. 147-57.

The Ministry is headed by a Cabinet Minister, who is assisted by a Deputy Minister. A Secretary and a Special Secretary in charge of Textiles, Plantations and certain other matters constitute the highest level in the permanent bureaucracy. The Secretary is assisted by nine Joint Secretaries and other secretarial staff. In addition, there are four Directors in charge of Export Assistance, Quality Control, Transport, and Commercial Publicity. Besides the office of the Chief Controller of Imports and Exports, which carries out decisions, the Ministry has also a number of Attached and Subordinate Offices, Advisory Bodies, and Trade Promotion Institutes.

Although originally the Ministry had six divisions, when it was reorganized in August 1947 the six were reduced to three: Administration and General, Internal Trade and Essential Supplies, and Foreign Commerce.

The Foreign Commerce Division has three Joint Secretaries, each heading one of the three wings: Establishment Policies or Economic Wing, Foreign Trade Development Wing, and the General Commercial Wing. Each Joint Secretary has over-all responsibility for his own wing and for coordination with the others. The General Commercial Wing, which deals primarily with the UN, has also a number of officials who look after their respective sections and work under the supervision of the Joint Secretary. It has five subdivisions responsible for GATT, UNCTAD, Tariffs, and Import and Export Trade Control. The GATT section, which is most important in regard to the UN, is headed by a Deputy Secretary, who is assisted by an Under Secretary, one Section Officer, and other staff. It has also a Special Officer for GATT and a Chief Research Officer. The ECAFE Cell has only an Under Secretary, one Section Officer, and clerical staff. The Cell was specially created as a result of the 1968 UNCTAD conference.

While the division of responsibility within the Ministry is fairly clear, work is shared and coordination is necessary. Ordinarily the briefs are prepared by the Foreign Commerce Division (especially the GATT research officers) and circulated within the Ministry. Frequent meetings of the Joint Secretaries are held to iron out differences. The Commerce Secretary, who has extensive experience with GATT and ECE, gives the final approval. Inter-ministerial coordination is also required. For example, briefs regarding international monetary issues prepared for the 1968 UNCTAD meeting were cleared with the Economic Department of the Ministry of Finance. Similarly, matters of political importance are subject to the approval of the Ministry of External Affairs. For example, decisions regarding the issuance of visas to the South African and Portuguese delegates to the UNCTAD meeting, whether the Indian delegates should join the walk-outs staged by the African delegates, and so forth, were made by the Ministry of External Affairs. Another important item which required similar decisions pertained to transit facilities for the commerce of land-locked countries, an item proposed by Nepal.

India is a member of the Trade and Development Board and has a permanent representative to GATT in Geneva. She also maintains contact with ECE through its Brussels Office, where a high official of the Government of India is posted. The annual meetings of GATT are ordinarily attended by the Minister of Commerce, who is assisted by the Secretary of the Ministry as alternate leader. The delegation also includes senior officials from the European-based offices, the Chief Controller of Imports and Exports, the Textile Commissioner, the Director General of Commercial Intelligence and Statistics, the President of the Indian Chamber of Commerce and Industry and representatives of some other ministries. The meetings of the Board are attended by the permanent representative. The Commerce Secretary presided over the GATT session in Geneva in 1967.

The UNCTAD meeting in New Delhi in 1968 was taken very seriously by the Indian Government. A steering comm ttee of Secretaries of several departments was formed to supervise the general arrangements. A general committee which included Joint Secretaries of all Ministries, private organizations such as the Indian Chamber of Commerce and Industry, Hoteliers and Air India, was also set up to look after certain details. The Conference Division in the Ministry of Commerce was responsible for the meetings. The interest of other Ministries was indicated by the composition of the Indian delegation, which was led by the Minister of Commerce, with the Minister of State in the Ministry of External Affairs and the Deputy Minister of Commerce as alternate leaders. It contained officials from the Ministries of Commerce, External Affairs, Finance, Industrial Development, Transport and Shipping, and Food and Agriculture, and four members of Parliament.

The separate Ministry of Commerce was intended to give greater attention to trade and commerce in order to increase foreign exchange for purposes of internal development. The success in the achievement of these objectives is to a certain extent dependent on the performance of other ministries. A permanent inter-departmental committee of Secretaries or their representatives, has been proposed to minimize delays in the implementation of the import and export program. Secondly, competent observers have recommended that the commercial sections of Indian Embassies abroad be manned by experts from the Ministry of Commerce rather than from the Foreign Service. In any case, there is a need to have experts rather than amateurs to look after India's commercial interests. It is also desirable that the Indian Government enlarge its office at Geneva so that it may efficiently serve GATT, UNCTAD, and other UN agencies.[47]

Ministry of Education

Under the Indian Constitution, education is a state subject. The Union government, however, is responsible for the maintenance of four Central Universities, institutions of national importance, others for professional, technical and vocational training, and for promotion of research coordination and determination of standards in higher education and research. Originally consisting of two departments—Education and Science—a composite Ministry of Education was established in 1965. It is headed by a Minister of Cabinet rank, who in 1967 was assisted by two Ministers of State. The Department has been reorganized into fourteen divisions, and these in turn into units.[48] Each Division is ordinarily headed by a Deputy Secretary or Deputy Educational Adviser, who is assisted by an Under Secretary and an Education Officer. The latter two are intermediate officers between the Deputy Secretary and the Section Officer. The latter is concerned with the day-to-day administration of the Division.

---

[47] S. K. Verghese, *Organization and Financing of India's Foreign Trade* (Unpublished Ph.D. Thesis of the University of Delhi, 1960), p. 425. The Mathur Committee Report on import and export trade reorganization has recommended that a regular central service to be known as *Indian Trade Service* should be constituted to provide for the needs of import and export trade control and that at a later stage the question of extending its scope to the Ministry of Commerce, GATT, etc. might be examined. *Report of the Study Team on Import and Export Trade Control Organization*. Pt. II, New Delhi: Directorate of Commercial Publicity, Ministry of Commerce, 1966, pp. 86, 119.

[48] Besides the main offices, there are 64 Attached and Subordinate offices and Autonomous Organizations: *Report 1966-67*, New Delhi: Ministry of Education, 1967, pp. 235-39.

Education, science and culture, as they relate to the UN, fall within the jurisdiction of the UNESCO Division of the Ministry. For a number of years this Division was headed by an officer of the rank of Deputy Secretary. Subsequently the incumbent was appointed head of the Asia Division in the Bureau of Relations with Member States of the UNESCO Secretariat in Paris. Afterward the position was left vacant, and for all practical purposes the Division is headed by an Under Secretary. The Chief reason for not filling the vacancy was that the incumbent Secretary of the Ministry of Education, through whom the work of all the divisions is channelled, had served UNESCO in many capacities, was quite familiar with its work, and therefore did not believe a higher officer was required.

The UNESCO Division is bifurcated into two units—the UNESCO Unit and the International Commission Unit (INC). The former's primary responsibility is the Government's relations with UNESCO, involving mainly questions of national policy and coordination. The functions of the latter are program execution in the field and providing secretarial assistance to the members of the Indian National Commission for UNESCO and its sub-commissions, as well as to committees and boards set up by the Minister of Education to work in close liaison with the Commission. One Under Secretary serves as head of both units. He is also designated Secretary of the Commission and in that capacity looks after the work of the INC. Although one common Under Secretary for both units seems to be conducive to efficiency and coordination, it is generally felt that the arrangement gives the Government too much control over the Commission.

Prior to 1962, since there was no separate Secretariat for the Commission, the UNESCO Unit of the Ministry served in that capacity. It was, however, felt that the arrangement was inappropriate, and in 1962 a separate staff was sanctioned for the purpose.[49] The staff of the INC consists of a full-time Secretary in the grade of Assistant Educational Officer, a Section Officer, four technical assistance, a librarian, a stenographer, four clerks, two steno-typists, one secretary and two messengers. The UNESCO Division as a whole has a strength of twenty-nine. The employees of the INC Unit are also at the same time the employees of the UNESCO Unit. It seems that they supplement each other's work.

Most of the responsibilities of the Ministry relating to UNESCO are delegated to the UNESCO Unit. It examines resolutions of the INC, and all correspondence with UNESCO or other international agencies is carried on by the Unit. There are cases, however, which are handled by some other divisions within the Ministry, though they concern UNESCO. For example, an agreement for a five-year joint project for reorganizing and expanding science education in schools, signed with UNESCO and UNICEF, was recently negotiated and approved by the Schools Division of the Ministry rather than by the UNESCO Division.[50] Similarly, other divisions may also be called upon to perform functions relating to UNESCO. Within the Ministry, however, the work is coordinated by the Secretary of the Ministry. Ordinarily the briefs are prepared by the UNESCO Division, in consultation with other divisions, and the views of other Ministries are procured when appropriate. If a question has "political" overtones, it is referred to the Ministry of External Affairs. For example, questions dealing with Israel, South Africa and Portugal are first cleared with the latter. If the subject falls within the jurisdiction of more than one ministry, discussions take place at the

---

[49] Indian National Commission for UNESCO: *Secretary General's Report 1960-63,* New Delhi: Ministry of Education, 1964, pp. 58-59.

[50] PTI Report, *The Times of India,* April 18, 1967.

Secretary level or a lower level, depending on its importance. For example, in 1967 a project for educational television through the use of satellites was being discussed with UNESCO. While the major responsibility was that of the All India Radio, Ministry of Information and Broadcasting, the Secretary of the Ministry of Education was kept informed of its status.[51]

Compared to other specialized agencies, UNESCO has found a rather favored place in the policies of the Indian Government. Indian delegates have played an important role in its deliberations, and from the beginning have served on its Executive Board. While India has been the recipient of much technical aid, she has also provided similar facilities to other developing countries. The calibre of the Indian delegations to UNESCO are indicative of the importance the Government attaches to the agency. Ordinarily the delegation to the annual conference is led by the Minister of Education, though on occasion the Minister of Information and Broadcasting, the Minister of Health, and even the Vice-President of India have served in that capacity. The Secretary of the Ministry of Education serves as Deputy Leader. Depending on the subject on the agenda, eminent educators have also been invited to serve on the delegation. The delegations also, it must be said, have had their share of politicians. In recent years, because of the tight foreign exchange situation, the delegations have been small, resulting in a considerable strain on the members as they are asked to attend meetings of a number of committees which meet at very close intervals. This has probably affected the efficiency of the delegates and they are unable to function as effectively as before.[52]

---

[51] *Ibid.* May 22, 1967.

[52] Indian National Commission for UNESCO: *Secretary General's Report 1964-65,* New Delhi: Ministry of Education, 1965, p. 30.

There appear to be three main defects in the handling of the UNESCO work by the Ministry of Education. In the first place, the UNESCO Unit is not properly staffed. A Deputy Secretary appointed to head the Division would provide the necessary expertise and relieve an already over-burdened Secretary. In any case, after the retirement of the present Secretary (who in 1967 was already on extension), a competent person would have to be appointed to head the Division. Secondly, the INC Unit should not be an integral part of the UNESCO Unit but should have a separate staff and be given broader competence in the formulation of policies. By making it an adjunct of the UNESCO Division, the INC has been reduced to the position of a mere advisory board, and has thus played a subordinate role. Lastly, the delegations to the international conferences should be larger and more broadly-based. In place of or in addition to the politicians and civil servants, more men of eminence in education, science and culture should be associated with the delegations as advisers. Moreover, the states should be properly represented. Most of the activities of UNESCO fall within the responsibility of the state governments. In the context of internal politics, the cooperation of state governments is essential in order that the decisions of the UNESCO may be properly implemented.

Ministry of Food, Agriculture, Community Development and Cooperation

The Ministry of Food, Agriculture, Community Development and Cooperation was brought into existence as a composite Ministry in 1966. Previously the Departments of Food and Agriculture had been included in a separate ministry as had those of Community Development and Cooperation. It was felt, however, that the subject matter of these organs was so closely related that coordination and administrative efficiency required their inclusion in a single ministry. The Ministry has a large number of attached and subordinate offices.[53] As of 1968, the Ministry was headed by a Minister of Cabinet rank, two Ministers of State and one Deputy Minister. One Secretary was in charge of the Department of Food, and another of the remaining three departments. The Department of Agriculture, however, had four Additional Secretaries, and Community Development and Cooperation one each.

All UN System activities falling within the jurisdiction of the Ministry are the primary responsibility of the Foreign Aid Division of the Department of Agriculture, one of its fifteen divisions.[54] The Foreign Aid Division is further subdivided into five sections.[55] The Foreign Aid: International Technical (FAIT) Section deals with international organizations concerned with activities in the agricultural field. This includes all technical aid in this sphere which may be given by FAO and other UN related agencies.

The Foreign Aid Division is under the general charge of an Additional Secretary, but for all practical purposes a Deputy Secretary, who also administers the FAIT Section, is the actual head. For this purpose he is assisted by an Under Secretary, a Section Officer, five Assistants, one Technical Assistant and three lower-division clerks. The major burden of running the FAIT Section, however, falls on the Under Secretary. The Deputy Secretary is also responsible for the other sections.

---

[53] For details regarding how these departments were organized up to 1957 see: *The Organization of the Government of India* (Bombay: Asia Publishing House, 1958), pp. 193-231; 329-33.

[54] The fifteen divisions are: General Administration; Foreign Aid; Lands; Fisheries; Minor Irrigation; Animal Husbandry; Forests Crops; Fertilizers; Seeds; Plant Protection; Machinery and Supplies; Personnel; Coordination; Farms.

[55] The five sections are: Foreign Aid: Bilateral (FAB); Foreign Aid: International Technical (FAIT); Foreign Aid National (FAN); Foreign Aid: Multilateral Economic (FAME); Foreign Aid: Evaluation Cell (FAEC).

All proposals regarding food and agriculture involving the UN System are considered in the Foreign Aid Division. Necessary recommendations relating to these matters, however are usually made by other divisions of different departments of the Ministry. For example, the proposal to establish fishery projects at Bombay, Madras, Mangalore, Tuticorn and Visakhapatnam, with the assistance of the World Bank, was first studied by the Fisheries Division of the Department of Agriculture. This Division has also been associated with the Foreign Aid Division for purposes of negotiation with the Ministry of Finance and the IBRD. The Foreign Aid Division depends to a great extent on the Directorate of Economics and Statistics for an intensive study of the problems before final decisions are made.[56] The latter is the sole organization in the Ministry charged with research on agro-economic problems. It prepares memoranda, special statements, reports for submissions to UN agencies, and briefs for the FAO Conference and for meetings of ILO, ECAFE, GATT, etc.

It is the responsibility of the Deputy Secretary to coordinate activities regarding FAO and other organizations within the Foreign Aid Division and also with other divisions. Occasionally meetings of the officials of the various divisions are held to decide strategies and to expedite action on the proposals. At times informal meetings or contacts via telephone with the officer concerned are deemed sufficient. Whenever desirable, *ad hoc* meetings of higher officials of the Ministry, especially of the Departments of Food and Agriculture, are called to decide priorities. Since agriculture, community development and cooperation are under the charge of a common Secretary,

---

[56] This office is headed by the Economic and Statistical Adviser who is an ex-officio Deputy Secretary to the Government of India. There are, in addition, about twenty-five Directors and Deputy Directors and twenty Research Officers.

clearance among them does not pose any serious problems

In order to give an impetus to agriculture, especially the production of food, the cooperation of a number of other ministries is necessary. The Ministries of Finance, Petroleum and Chemicals, Industry, Commerce, Shipping and the Planning Commission, as well as others are also directly or indirectly concerned with the problem. Coordination among these departments is achieved through occasional meetings of the Departmental Secretaries or their deputies.[57] Just as FAO cooperates with a number of other UN agencies for the provision of facilities in different spheres, the Ministry of Food and Agriculture is required to collaborate with other ministries or secure clearance from them on matters of mutual concern. For example, in 1964, FAO signed an agreement with IBRD to set up a joint program to help developing countries identify and prepare projects which the latter might consider financing. In order to take advantage of such facilities, the Ministry of Food and Agriculture required the cooperation of the Ministry of Finance which handles work relating to IBRD and its subsidiaries. Since FAO has similar arrangements with many other international agencies, the Ministry seeks the cooperation of the departments of the Indian government primarily responsible for relations with such agencies.

Items which concern other ministries are first referred to them for comment. Sometimes two or even three ministries may be interested in the program, but the initiative may rest with one ministry. For example, in the case of the Applied Nutrition Program, the Ministry of Health has also been interested. Similarly, steps are

---

[57] *Report 1966-67*, New Delhi: Department of Agriculture, 1967, p. 5.

taken to secure close coordination at the operational level between the Applied Nutrition Program and the program of Mid-day Meal and Family and Child Welfare sponsored by the Ministry of Education and the Department of Social Welfare. On the whole, where problems of money are concerned, the approval of the Ministry of Finance is necessary as is indicated by the cases of loans for agriculture advanced by the World Bank. On political matters, the prior approval of the Ministry of External Affairs is sought. For example, the briefs on agenda items of the Fourteenth FAO Conference relative to the Indicative World Plans for Agricultural Development and amendment to Article VI relative to the Sea-area Fishery Commission were referred to it for approval.

India was one of the founding members of the FAO and has taken a keen interest in its deliberations. She has been frequently elected to membership in the Council, has a seat on the Committee on Commodity Problems, is a member of the Advisory Committee for the Freedom from Hunger Campaign to represent the Far Eastern Region, and is a member of the Finance Committee of the Organization. In order to participate effectively in the meetings of these committees, India has maintained a permanent office at FAO Headquarters in Rome. This office, which is under the control of the Indian Embassy there, is headed by a Deputy Secretary from the Ministry of Food and Agriculture who is assisted by a small staff. The meetings of the Council and the various committees are attended by the permanent representative, who is also assisted by the Agricultural Counsellor of the Indian Embassy. At times a higher official from the Ministry may attend the meeting if important items appear on the agenda. In 1967, for example, the Additional Secretary in Charge of the Foreign Aid Division attended the Council's meetings.

The Conference of FAO is generally attended by a high-level delegation led by the Minister of Food and Agriculture or by his Deputy. This may include a Minister of Agriculture from one of the Indian states, high officials of the Ministry, technical experts in the various fields, representatives of other Ministries whenever desirable, and the Agricultural Counsellor of the Indian Embassy in Rome.[58] Because of the shortage of foreign exchange, however, the number of personnel sent abroad for such meetings is rather small and only important meetings are attended by Indian representatives.

The administrative arrangements seem to be generally satisfactory. It is probably desirable, however, that a higher official should head the FAIT Section so that decisions may be made expeditiously and delays avoided. As the FAO Regional Office for Asia and the Far East is located in New Delhi, most of the day-to-day negotiations with the FAO can be carried on either through telephone or by personal visits. Since this is the case, the permanent mission in Rome may be closed or handled by the Agricultural Counsellor in the Embassy, and the Foreign Aid Division, especially the section on FAO, strengthened. Though nothing has been done in this direction, the Indian government has an open mind on rationalizing procedures, assessing staff requirements and increasing efficiency. In order to cater to the needs of food and agriculture and for effective implementation of the various programs, the Ministry of Food and Agriculture is frequently reorganized to achieve maximum utilization

---

[58] In the 1967 Conference, the following persons represented India: Minister of Food and Agriculture; Minister of Food and Revenue, Madras; Additional Secretary, Ministry of Food and Agriculture; Agricultural Counsellor, Indian Embassy, Rome; Additional Economic and Statistical Adviser; Maharaja of Patiala; Executive Director, Department of Food; Agricultural Commissioner; Inspector General of Forests; Joint Secretary (Factories) and Private Secretary to the Minister.

of personnel. Special efforts are being made so that the agricultural program, which is assisted by FAO, may be expeditiously implemented and necessary results achieved.

Ministry of Labour, Employment and Rehabilitation

India is an original member of ILO, and as one of the member states with considerable industry she enjoys permanent membership on the Governing Body. Moreover she has showed enthusiasm for the work of the organization, which at least partly accounts for the establishing of an ILO Branch Office in New Delhi in 1928.

As in the case of education, labor is primarily a state subject under the Indian federal system. Although there is no legal obstacle to central enforcement of ILO conventions, as a political and administrative reality the Centre has to rely heavily on the cooperation of the states in such matters. A number of labor subjects, however, is included in the concurrent list—those on which either the Centre or the states may legislate—with primacy given to the Centre in case of conflict. Generally speaking, the result is that the Union Government exercises over-all responsibility in matters of labor welfare, employment, training, etc. To that end the Ministry establishes national policies in regard to working conditions relating to safety and health, industrial disputes, and regulation of wages.

Within the Ministry the ILO Division, one of five, has the chief responsibility for ILO matters. Prior to 1957, it was known as Division C. Later it has been somewhat misleadingly referred to as the Labour Conference Section and Research Division. The Section deals with the more important matters, such as arranging meetings, selecting delegations, and deciding policy, whereas the Division's functions are of a more technical nature, including the collection and compilation of material for briefs for government delegations and follow-up action

on the Conventions and recommendations. The Division
is concerned with both national and international problems within the purview of the entire Ministry.[59]

The Labour Conference Section and Research Division is headed by an officer with the rank of Deputy Secretary. He is assisted by two Under Secretaries, one serving as head of the Labour Conference Section and the
other of the Research Division. There are, in addition,
two Section officers, six assistants and eight clerks and
steno-typists.

Since India is a permanent member of the ILO Governing Board, in 1956 the Government created the post
of Labour Attaché, later redesignated as International Labour Adviser, in the Indian Consulate-General in
Geneva. By his continued presence at ILO Headquarters,
the Adviser has been able to establish contacts with

---

[59] In the international sphere, the Research Division is responsible for:
1. Collection and compilation of material on the position of
   India in ILO for publications.
2. Replying to ILO Questionnaires concerning labour subjects.
3. Preparation of 'Briefs' for Government Delegations attend-
   ing ILO Conferences, Governing Body Sessions and the
   ILO Industrial and Analogous Committees.
4. Bringing out the Report of the Indian Delegation to the
   Annual Sessions of the International Labour Conference.
5. Follow-up action on the Conventions, Recommendations
   and Resolutions adopted by the International Labour Conference and the ILO Industrial and Analogous Committees.
6. Carrying out the obligation arising out of India's membership in the ILO; preparation of the "Statement of
   Parliament" in respect of Conventions and Recommendations adopted by the International Labour Conference.
7. Work in respect of the UN Bodies like the General Assembly, ECOSOC, UNESCO, and ECAFE insofar as the
   labour matters are concerned.
8. Distribution of ILO Publications.
(Information supplied by the Ministry *Vide* D.O., No. RD.
225 (383), 67).

representatives of governments, employers and workers of different shades of opinion. He has also utilized his time between meetings to make on-the-spot studies of labor welfare in European countries. In 1962, however, Dr. S. T. Merani, who held this job with distinction for a number of years, was recalled and the post was still vacant in 1968. It seems that the tight foreign exchange situation in India and the various economy measures followed by the Government dictated this decision. The work formerly performed by the Labour Adviser was subsequently carried on by the Indian Consulate-General in Geneva.

Ordinarily the initiative for most of the activities comes from the ILO Governing Board which sends the proposals to member countries. The Indian Government passes these on to the Ministry of Labour where they are studied by the Research Division with a view to preparing notes and briefs. The latter are then passed on to the Labour Conference Section where the necessary decisions are made. If an item has "political" ramifications, guidance from the Ministry of External Affairs is sought. For example, "political" decisions with respect to the Declaration on Apartheid and a program of action for the elimination of racial discrimination in the Union of South Africa, as well as the movement for expulsion of Portugal from the ILO, were made by that Ministry. Similarly, matters involving financial commitments were cleared with the Ministry of Finance. For example, the Government of India decided to press for reduced contribution to the ILO by the developing countries, and the Secretary of the Ministry of Labour who attended the budget session of the ILO was asked to pursue the matter in the General Conference.[60] It is apparent that such a decision must have the prior approval of the Ministry of Finance. Likewise the Ministry of Health was consulted on the

---

[60] *The Times of India* (New Delhi), 17 February 1967, p. 2.

move of the delegates of India and Sweden to sponsor a resolution urging that the ILO Conference prepare a plan for assisting developing countries in their family planning programs. In most of cases intra-and inter-ministerial coordination is achieved either by telephone, by correspondence or through meetings at the Secretary level. Ordinarily the head of the Division concerned accompanies the Secretary.

The Indian Government has also established a number of advisory bodies composed of representatives of central organizations of employers, workers, state governments, and the Union Government to discuss labor problems and to make recommendations to the Union Government. The Indian Labour Conference, which meets annually, studies promotion of uniformity in labor legislation, lays down a procedure for the settlement of industrial disputes, and discusses matters of general importance arising between employers and employees, including matters relating to labor welfare and the maintenance of labor morality. The Standing Labour Committe examines and considers such questions as may be referred to it by the Indian Labour Conference or by the Indian Government, taking into account the suggestions made by the State governments and representative organs of employers and workers. Similarly, a Committee on Conventions usually composed of representatives of central organizations of workers, employers, state governments (now discontinued) and the Union Government has been in existence since 1954.[61] It examines and reviews ILO Conventions and Recommendations and makes proposals for their approval or disapproval. Since these bodies are

---

[61] *The Organization of the Government of India,* p. 190.
It should be noted that the officials of the Research Division did not have any knowledge regarding state representation in the Committee on Conventions. Their attention, however, was drawn to the above publication.

purely advisory, the Government is not bound by their recommendations.[62]

Ordinarily the Union Minister of Labour, or his counterpart from some state, heads the delegation to the General Conference. He usually makes the major speech on behalf of the Government. Unless there are very important items on the agenda, the Minister returns to India, leaving the delegation to be headed by an official, ordinarily the Secretary of the Ministry. There have been cases, however, where the Secretary of the Ministry of Industries has served as the leader. The other members of the delegation are ordinarily officials from the Centre or the States. For example, they have included the Commissioner of Burdwan Division, Bengal; a member of the

---

[62] The actual procedure followed by the Government of India in pursuance of Article 19 of the ILO Constitution regarding Conventions, etc., is as follows:

The texts of all the instruments adopted at any given session of the International Labour Conference are printed as appendices to the Report of the Indian Government Delegation to the particular session of the Conference. This Report is placed before the Parliament of India as soon as possible. Simultaneously, copies of the Conventions and Recommendations are circulated to the State Governments, the employing Ministries of the Government of India as well as the all-India organizations of workers and employers, inviting their views regarding the desirability and practicability of giving effect to these instruments in toto or in part. The texts of these instruments are also placed for consideration before the Tripartite Committee on Conventions, which was set up by the Government of India in 1954 to advise Government regarding the implementation of international labor standards. A statement of action proposed to be taken is then drawn up, taking into account the various comments received, and placed before the Union Parliament with the approval of the Cabinet. Members of Parliament are free to raise a discussion on the proposals contained in the Statement. Copies of the Statement are thereafter forwarded to the International Labour Office, the State Governments and the employers' and workers' organizations, etc. Follow-up action by way of ratification of Conventions, etc., is then taken.

Railway Board; the Director of Labour Conferences; and Secretaries of the Labour Departments of the various state governments. Since, 1960, however, the delegations have been smaller than before, again because of foreign exchange stringencies.[63]

The meetings of the Governing Board are attended by the Secretary of Labour, or the Deputy Secretary in charge of the ILO Division. Quite often a Secretary from the Indian Embassy in Berne, or an official from the Indian Consulate-General, Geneva, attends meetings of the General Board and its committees. For special meetings the Indian government may appoint some official with the necessary expertise. For example, the Technical Maritime Conference of the ILO, held in London, was attended by the Director General of Shipping as leader of a tripartite delegation.

On the whole the various arrangements to further Indian foreign policy in labor matters have been satisfactory. The discontinuance of the job of Labour Attaché in Geneva, however, has its drawbacks. Indian policy suffers from lack of expert representation at ILO headquarter, although on policy matters the Indian Embassy and the Consulate-General may fill the gap. India has also been one of the major providers of technical assistance through ILO. Though some negotiations may be conducted through the ILO office in New Delhi and the regional office in Bangkok, the permanent posting of an officer a Geneva will probably pay in the long run.

India has so far ratified only thirty Conventions. In order that greater progress be made, it is desirable that the states play a more active role in the formulation of policies regarding labor matters. Specifically, the former

---

[63] *Report of the Indian Government Delegation to the 50th Session o the International Labour Conference Geneva, June, 1966,* New Delhi: Government of India Press, 1967, p. 14.

practice of including state representatives on the Committee on Conventions should be resumed.[64]

Ministry of Health and Family Planning

The two Departments of the Ministry of Health and Family Planning and its many related organs are responsible for formulating policy, and for administering and supervising the administration of a wide range of UN-assisted programs. Although their primary concern is with WHO, both in Geneva and at its India Office, several other UN organs are involved in the health program.

Matters relating to WHO are dealt with primarily by the International Health Relations Division of the Department of Health, one of its five divisions, each headed by a Deputy Secretary. Within the International Relations Division, the WHO Section, under the control of an Under Secretary, with a total strength of nine, carries on most of the work relating to that agency. There is, however, no strict delineation of functions. For example, the Fellowship Section, which is controlled by the Under Secretary who also heads the WHO Section, serves more or less as an adjunct of the latter. The two sections, having a total staff of seventeen, for all practical purposes work as one office.

Besides the Secretariat arrangement, the Department is assisted by the Office of the Director General of Health Services which functions as the chief executive organization for the Ministry in the entire medical and public health field. The Director General holds the rank of Secretary. He is assisted by eight Deputy Secretaries General and a number of Assistant Deputy Directors General and Directors. In addition, he has advisers on venereal

---

[64] At present the Committee consists of the Labour Secretary (Chairman) and two other members—one representing each the employers and workers.

diseases, T. B., nutrition, nursing, maternity and child welfare, and medical education, as well as on a few other matters. The Department also has a number of subordinate offices and advisory bodies. Although policy matters are the responsibility of the Secretariat, on technical matters the Ministry of Health is guided by the Director General of Health Services.

The Director General, who is in continuous contact with the Secretary of the Department of Health, supervises field operations. These include WHO and UNICEF aided programs such as the National Malaria Eradication Scheme, as well as others dealing with smallpox, trachoma, and cholera. The Director General has direct access to the field offices of the respective UN agencies in India.[65]

Besides the International Health Relation Division, several others units are also in the picture. The Drugs Controls Organization, supervised by the Drugs and Stores Division, has close liaison with WHO. Similarly, liaison with other ministries is also maintained. For example, in their campaign against spurious drugs, the Police Department in the Ministry of Home Affairs has nominated a senior officer to work with the Drug Control Authorities. The National School Health Council, reconstituted in April, 1966, to develop a health care program, including school mid-day meals, coordinates its work with the Schools Division of the Ministry of Education. The Ministry of Health and Family Planning also coordinates activities under the Emergency Programme for water supply in drought-affected areas by meeting with representatives of the Ministry of Food and Agriculture, and the Indian based offices of UNICEF, WHO, and USAID.[66]

---

[65] See *Report 1966-67*, New Delhi: Ministry of Health and Family Planning, 1967, pp. 8-50.

[66] *Ibid*, pp. 102-03.

The sanitary control of maritime and aerial traffic, particularly the prevention of spread of quarantinable diseases from one country to another, is regulated under the Indian Port Health Rules (1955) and the Indian Aircraft (Public Health) Rules (1954), which are based on International Sanitary Regulations provided by WHO. These are enforced by the Ministry through its subordinate offices known as Seaports and Airports Health Organizations. As international quarantine is a central subject, the quarantine administration at the six major shipping ports and five international airports is directly under the control of the central government. The quarantine administration at the minor ports has been delegated to the respective state governments which have established Health Education Bureaus with the assistance of the Union Government. WHO and UNICEF have made available equipment and supplies for these Bureaus. At the instance of the Ministry of Health, the Director General, Civil Aviation, has issued instructions to Aerodrome authorities to incorporate standard health clauses in the agreements pertaining to lease of airport land to other parties for the purpose of maintaining public health at the airports.

In April 1966, a separate Department of Family Planning was established in the Ministry of Health and Family Planning in order to give greater attention to population control.[67] The Secretariat Wing deals with policy matters concerning family planning and the coordination of the work between the states and central agencies, and between them and the appropriate international agencies. The Technical Wing, headed by the Commissioner of Family Planning, renders technical advice and looks after field operations relating to family planning. Although the Family Planning Department deals with the India-based offices

---

[67] *Ibid,* p. 200.

of the Specialized Agencies, ordinarily negotiations on important matters are first cleared with the International Relations Divisions of the Department of Health. Since the two Departments have a common Secretary, coordination and clearance is a simple matter. Because of the importance of the problem, a Cabinet Sub-Committee considers policy matters. A number of other ministries— Finance, Labour, Education, Community Development, and Information and Broadcasting—are also approached to assist in the achievement of the goals. Coordination, however is primarily at the initiative of the Ministry of Health and Family Planning.

India was an original member of WHO, and served on its Executive Board for a number of years. Though the Minister of Health and Family Planning and his counterparts in the various state governments often head the delegations to important conferences, the membership of these delegations is overwhelmingly professional. Dr. A. L. Mudaliar, an eminent physician and Vice-Chancellor of Madras University, has quite frequently served as leader of the delegation. Others who have served on the delegations at one time or the other are the Dirctor General of Health Services; Director, Indian Council of Medical Research; Secretary, Indian Cancer Society; Director, All India Institute of Hygiene and Public Health, and other experts in different branches of medicine. At times eminent medical doctors who are members of Parliament are also invited to serve as advisers. The Secretary, Union Ministry of Health and Family Planning, and Director General of Health Services have also attended the meetings of the Executive Board of WHO and UNICEF. The Secretaries of the Departments of Health in the various State Governments are also frequently included in the delegation.[68]

---

[68] For the list of delegates to the 19th World Health Assembly held at Geneva see, *ibid,* pp. 232-33.

The arrangements on the whole are quite satisfactory. The lack of sufficient staff in the secretariat of the Ministry is met by relying on the technicians in the Directorate of Health Services. It should be noted, however, that the Under Secretary of the WHO Section for all practical purposes controls the working of the International Relations Division and for some time no Deputy Secretary has been assigned this work. Unless a senior officer is appointed, it seems probable that efficiency will be affected and decisions delayed. As of December, 1966, fifty-six projects were being financed by WHO in India, in addition to a number of inter-country projects.[69] It is desirable that necessary administrative arrangements be provided so that these may be effectively prosecuted.

---

[69] *Ibid,* pp. 266-31. WHO provided $910,453 under the regular Budget, and $1,193,561 under its technical assistance budget for the implementation of its programs, in India during 1966. During 1967, WHO has provided $1,493,894 under its regular Budget and $980,649 under its technical assistance budget.

6

India's Permanent UN Mission and General Assembly Delegations

The composition of various delegations to UN System conferences has been described in the discussion of the work of the ministries and other government bodies. It has been noted that for the most part the delegations consist of both permanent and political members of the concerned organs of the Union Governments, and in several instances of the states as well. All of these delegations are *ad hoc*. Several of the UN organs require almost continuous representation, but except for UN Headquarters, the Bank "family" and GATT, this is provided on a part-time basis by the regular diplomatic missions stationed in the various countries.

There remains for consideration only the Permanent Mission to UN Headquarters and the delegation to the General Assembly. Although India's permanent UN Mission is small in absolute numbers, it is larger than that of all but a dozen or so of the other UN members. In 1965 there were thirteen members of the Mission and in each of the two subsequent years fifteen persons were officially listed as members. In addition to these officials, the Mission was assisted by approximately thirty-five clerks, messengers, and similar types of personnel. Thus the total staff consisted of approximately fifty persons.

The Head of the Mission, with the rank of Ambassador, is India's Permanent Representative to the UN. He represents India in the Security Council when she is a member of that organ, serves as a member of the delegation to the General Assembly, and is in charge of the work of the Mission generally. He has always been a high-ranking member of the Indian Foreign Service.

The average tenure of office has been approximately three years. The Permanent Representative in 1968, Mr. Gopalaswami Parthasarathi, was first appointed to the position in 1965. Since 1966, the second in command has been the Deputy Permanent Representative, with the rank of Counsellor. These two, plus a number of First Secretaries, four in 1965, six in 1966, and seven in 1967, have, aside from the Assembly Delegations, been responsible for representing India in the various UN Headquarters meetings and in conducting Indian diplomacy in New York. A number of other staff members, such as military and press advisers, also with the rank of First Secretary, and attachés, who serve as research officers, round out the professional side of the staff. In 1967, four of the six research officers were members of the IFS (B), and the remaining two were Indian students residing in the United States working for graduate degrees in American universities.

Although the principal officers participate in the general activities of the Mission, the seven First Secretaries also specialize in particular phases of the work. Ordinarily one First Secretary is chiefly responsible for administration, whereas each of the remaining six concentrates on a different set of problems. These are: political and disarmament; special political questions; human rights and social; colonial and trusteeship; budget and finance; and legal and treaties. The research officers also tend to specialize in these fields and to backstop the First Secretaries.

The delegations to the General Assembly have ranged in size from a low of nineteen in the Second Session (1947) to a high of thirty-four in the Twenty-Second (1967). The Chairman of the delegation is usually the Minister for External Affairs, although in 1967 the Defense Minister, Swaran Singh, was the head. The explanation for this departure from normal practice was that the Foreign Minister had recently resigned and the Prime Minister had taken over the portfolio. Since it did not seem desirable for her to chair the delegation, it was appropriate that the Defense Minister do so for he had previously served as Chairman when he was Foreign Minister prior to the Fourth General Elections of 1967. It is also customary for the Permanent Representative to serve as one of the five Representatives. In three of the four delegations to the Nineteenth through the Twenty-Second Session, from one to all of the remaining three Representatives have been Indian Ambassadors to European countries. In each of the three years the Ambassador to Switzerland had been included. The Union Minister for Commerce and three Ministers from the states have also served as Representatives. Although members of Parliament have not served as Representatives, from three to six have been included in the delegations either as alternate Representatives or as Parliamentary Advisers.

There seems to be no discernible pattern in the selection of Alternate Representatives. Members of Parliament, the Deputy Permanent Representative Union Ministers, Consuls General, Ambassadors, Ministers of Embassy, representatives of the Ministry of External Affairs, and others have served in that capacity.

In addition to the ten Representatives and Alternate Representatives, from 1964 through 1967 the delegations have consisted of from seventeen to twenty-five advisers. The number of Parliamentary Advisers, i.e., members of Parliament, has varied from three in 1964 to six in 1967. The vast majority of the others have been members of the Permanent Mission, seven in 1964, fifteen in 1965 and eighteen in 1966 and 1967.

India has continuously and actively participated in the meetings of the Afro-Asian and Asian groups at the United Nations on all issues of common interest. The African and Asian groups are primarily concerned with formulating a common stand on elections to the various organs of the United Nations, whereas the Afro-Asian group is the main political forum for evolving a common strategy. The Asian group, unlike its African counterpart, however, does not resort to voting in deciding the nomination of candiates from this region. Instead it endorses candidates only if there is unanimous agreement.

The meetings of the Afro-Asian group are usually held on two types of occasions: first, to exchange views on the procedural aspects of important agenda items before the opening of the regular sessions of the General Assembly; and secondly, to consider a common line of action on individual agenda items during committee debate or in plenary sessions. The latter usually takes place in connection with drafting resolutions in the concluding stages of the discussion of a particular question.

Close contacts are also maintained with the Latin-American group, especially on economic and trade matters which are of special interest to the developing nations. On legal issues, the Indian Mission maintains contacts with the representatives of other like-minded nations, including those of both Western and Eastern member states.

The delegation of India participates actively in caucusing groups on issues considered by the main committees of the General Assembly, as well as by its standing committees, such as the Committee of Twenty-four, the Committee of Thirty-three (on peace-keeping), the Committee on Friendly Relations, etc. The participation is both at the level of individuals and of groups.

Like other Missions, the Indian Mission also receives both general and specific instructions on all agenda items before the UN organs. The scope of these instructions naturally varies according to the nature of the problem and the circumstances prevailing in each case. In case of new or unexpected developments, the Mission seeks confirmation or fresh guidance from New Delhi. However, a majority of the issues discussed at the UN being more or less of a continuing nature, the need for detailed and elaborate instructions is obviated. Important and sometimes unforeseen developments do, however, take place, in which case instructions are sought or recommendations made to New Delhi.

How important is the Mission and Delegation in the formulation of policy positions? It is difficult to be precise on this question, or to give concrete illustrations, for the shaping of policy position is a long-term process in which many factors are considered by several groups at different levels. Nevertheless, it is agreed, both in New Delhi and in New York, that the Mission and Delegation do have some influence.

Like other missions and delegations, those of India serve as the eyes and ears of the home government as well as its mouthpiece. While India takes an active part in issues which are of special interest to the developing countries, this does not mean a lack of interest in others. For this reason the Mission keeps an especially close contact with the leading members of other regional groups, as well as with the Permanent Members of the Security Council.

If one were to single out the most important general aspect of the Mission's work, "it would be the maintenance of close and friendly contacts with as many delegations as possible. This, after all, is the essence of multilateral diplomacy at the United Nations and its utility is beyond any doubt."[70]

Throughout the entire period of its activity at the UN, the Indian Mission has endeavoured to strengthen the role of the UN in the maintenance of peace and security and has cooperated with other states in evolving acceptable procedures and formulae for the settlement of several international problems which are well-known. One particular recent instance may be mentioned. This concerns the role of the delegation in contributing to the adoption of the Security Council resolution of November 22, 1967, which laid the framework for a settlement of the West Asian (Middle Eastern) crisis. In this case India played an active role in working out a common position, first among Afro-Asians and Latin-Americans, and then with other non-permanent members of the Security Council.

---

[70] Statement of a First Secretary in the Permanent Mission.

7

India's Contributions to The United Nations System

India has been a major beneficiary of the UN social and economic programs, but she has also made important contributions, some of which, especially in the area of technical assistance, have been noted above. Indians have also held many high positions in both the UN itself and in the Specialized Agencies, and contributions to the Secretariat, peace-keeping activities, and technical assistance have been substantial and important.

Indian leaders have been consistent in their attitude that the Secretariat should be a truly international institution, and that the primary allegiance of its staff should be to the world organization. It was in this spirit that India rejected the Troika Plan which would have made the proposed Secretaries-General responsible to their respective groups rather than to the larger community. Nor does the Indian government attempt any kind of screening or "loyalty" test for Indians who are employed by the UN. Perhaps in "leaning over backward" in this respect the government may be less helpful than it might otherwise have been.

With regard to the composition of the UN Secretariat, India has advocated a blending of selection based on merit with the widest possible distribution of staff on a geographical basis. In both these categories she has been in an advantageous position, especially with regard to the other Asian states. Though North America and Europe have provided the bulk of the personnel, Indians have also received a substantial share of the positions. As a matter of fact, it has been charged that she is over-represented in the Secretariat: that of forty per cent of the senior jobs allotted to Asia, eleven posts of Director and above and more than half of the positions in the senior category for the Asian and Far Eastern region have been held by Indian nationals.[71]

There is some truth in these charges. From the very beginning of the UN, a considerable number of Indians were recruited to fill positions in the Secretariat, and over the years more have been added.[72] This is due, in part, to the fact that the region as a whole is somewhat over-represented. For example, as of 1967, out of the total number of positions to be filled on a geographical basis, personnel from the Asian and Far Eastern Region filled 296 or 16.5 per cent; the "Desirable Range" was 245-248. Indian nationals filled the largest number of these positions (66) in the region, even though the "Desirable Range" was substantially lower (19-25). (See Table I, page 91). India's position, moreover, has remained more or less stationary for the last few years, even though the Secretary General has followed the policy of adjusting

---

[71] Pakistan's representative in the Fifth Committee, *The Dawn*, November 2, 1966.

[72] For a comparative table see: *The Year Book of the United Nations 1948-49*, p. 909.

positions on a geographical basis.[73] The Indian representatives on the Fifth Committee have insisted that the Secretary General should be given the necessary latitude so that merit would not be sacrificed in implementing General Assembly resolutions to bring about equitable geographical representation.[74]

In conformity with the General Assembly directives, the Secretary General decided that each member state should have the right to a minimum of one to five nationals in the Secretariat, and that in allotting the posts he would keep in mind the regional distribution of population and the scale of assessment paid by the member concerned.[75] It is felt that this formula represents a marked improvement over the earlier exclusive reliance on financial contributions. Though Indian representation may be somewhat reduced over the years as more qualified candidates are available from other states of the region, India is bound to be heavily represented because of her financial contribution and population. Moreover, she has a large number of qualified persons who can effectively compete on the basis of merit. Out of the 131 Indians who, as of August 31, 1967 worked for the UN, more than half had been selected on the basis of open competition.[76]

---

[73] It is understood that the reduction would have to be made from fixed term appointments at the end of the term. But there does not seem to be any change. See the following figures:

Fixed Term Staff in Professional and Higher Level Posts Subject to Geographical Distribution

India:	1963	1964	1965	1966	1967
	18	13	14	16	18

[74] A/c.5/SR.1049 (20 November 1963), par. 11.
[75] Resolutions: A/1852 & 2241.
[76] A/C.5/L.900/Add. 1, *Report of the Secretary General* (November 2, 1967, pp. 57-58.

That Indians may be over-represented in the Secretariat is certainly not because of any pressure by the Indian Government. There is no central recruiting agency and, according to officials in the UN Division of the Ministry of External Affairs, the Government has no record of the Indians serving in the UN System civil

TABLE I

Staff in Professional and Higher Level Posts Subject to Geographical Distribution as of 31. 8. 1967

Country	U-2	D-2	D-1	P-5	P-4	P-3	P-2	P-1	Total	Desirable Range
Australia	x	2	1	5	4	4	4	3	23	21-17
Burma	1	x	x	2	6	3	x	1	13	2-5
Cambodia	x	x	x	x	x	1	2	1	4	2-5
Ceylon	x	x	1	1	6	4	2	x	14	2-6
China	1	3	5	12	11	8	10	6	56	55-38
India	1	3	6	18	24	7	7	x	66	25-19
Indonesia	x	x	1	1	4	3	4	1	14	6-8
Japan	x	x	1	1	10	15	5	1	33	36-26
Laos	x	x	x	x	x	x	2	1	3	2-5
Malaysia	x	x	x	x	x	2	x	2	4	2-5
Nepal	x	x	x	x	1	3	2	x	6	2-5
New Zealand	1	x	3	2	5	x	2	x	13	6-8
Pakistan	x	x	1	4	4	5	x	3	17	6-8
Philippines	x	x	x	2	6	4	3	1	16	5-8
Singapore	x	x	x	x	x	x	x	1	1	2-5
Thailand	x	x	x	x	3	5	1	4	13	3-6

Source: *U.N.* A/6860, p. 7.

services. When the Government is approached for nominations to fill top-level jobs, ordinarily it calls upon officials from the Centre or state services. In other cases a particular ministry may advertise a job and simply forward all applications, without comment, to the UN authorities.

India is especially proud of her major contributions to the UN peace-keeping forces: she has contributed more troops than any other state to both UNEF and ONUC operations. As of 1962, of the total of 5,133 men in the

UNEF, 1,249 were Indians. Canadians, the second largest force, numbered 945 (See Table II, below). When the UNEF was withdrawn in April 1967, India's contingent numbered 998. Altogether a total of approximately fifteen thousand Indians served in the West Asian UNEF force over a ten-year period. Although India did not supply military forces at the time of the crises in Lebanon and Yemen, she did furnish a number of military advisers.

TABLE II

Consolidated Strength of the UNEF on 22. 8. 1962

Contingent	Officers	Other Ranks	Total
Brazil	40	590	630
Canada	82	863	945
Denmark	45	517	562
India	80	1169	1249
Norway	84	529	613
Sweden	33	391	424
Yugoslavia	68	642	710
			5133

U.N. Doc. A/5172, p. 5.

UNEF Strength in 1967

Brazil (Infantry Unit)	455
Canada (Service Unit)	783
Scandinavia Countries (Infantry and medical)	602
India (Infantry)	998
Yugoslavia	562
Total	3400

UNEF, *Facts Sheet,* (Beirut) File No. PR. 200. Issued by Public Information Office, H. Q. UNEF.

India's most substantial contribution of personnel was made to the Congo operations. Of a total of approximately 16,000 men in the ONUC force as of May, 1962, over six thousand were Indian. Ethiopia, the second largest contributor, had about half that number. (See Table III, below). India also established and manned a 400-bed hospital in the Congo on behalf of the UN.

TABLE III

ONUC Troops Contingent of Countries which Provided the Largest Number of Troops (as of 5 May 1962)

Country	Staff	Troops	Air	Adm.	Total
Canada	23	xxxx	15	270	308
Ethiopia	14	2952	52	xxx	3018
India	42	5151	135	866	6194
Nigeria	5	1637	xxx	xxx	1642
Tunisia	2	1047	xxx	xxx	1049
Malaya	9	1509	xxx	xxx	1518
Sweden	15	781	149	72	1017
Pakistan	29	xxxx	xxx	651	680
Ghana	2	672	xxx	xxx	674

Source: D. W. Bowett, *United Nations Forces* (London: Stevens, 1964), p. 206.

In Cyprus, the Secretary General appointed an Indian, Gen. P. S. Gyani as the Commander of the UN troops, and upon his resignation in June, 1964, Gen. Thimayya another Indian, succeeded him. Gen. Inderjit Rikhe, who had previously served as military adviser to the Secretary General, served as Commander of the UN troops in the Congo. Mr. Rajeshwar Dayal, later a Secretary of the Ministry of External Affairs, was appointed Special Representative of the Secretary General in the Congo in September 1960. All told, it may be said that India has provided the largest number of troops to keep the peace and has, in general, shown enthusiasm for peace-keeping activities of the UN. Unlike some of the Scandinavian countries, however, she has not ear-marked any military units for that purpose.

India has also been one of the largest providers of technical aid under UN auspices. From 1951 to 1967, she provided approximately 2,000 experts to serve in various countries under the UNDP program and its predecessors. During the same period some 1,800 foreign experts worked in India under the same program.[77] In 1967 there were 250 Indian technical assistant experts engaged in UN and Specialized Agency projects in Asia, Africa, and Latin America. India has also received "thousands of fellows in various scientific fields, including education, administration, community development and agriculture." It is clear, therefore, that India "is one of the largest repositories of expertise of UNDP projects throughout the world."[78] A number of higher officials have been called upon by the Secretary General to work for the UN in key positions. Indians like to think that this expression of confidence is based on India's devotion to the UN ideals, a reputation for impartiality and objectivity, and a desire to make the UN a success.

That India's contributions of men have been greater than those of money is understandable. Men are plentiful in India and money is scarce. Although India's 1966 assessment was only 1.85 per cent of the regular UN budget, amounting to $2,124,327, this represented the tenth largest assessment among all the UN members. Moreover, she has been quite prompt in paying the amounts assessed. Total contributions to the Specialized Agencies have been considerably greater than to the regular UN budget. In 1967, for example, they amounted to $879,300 to WHO, $653,947 to ILO, $579,069 to FAO, and $520,730 to UNESCO. India has also made generous contributions to UNICEF, amounting to more than a million dollars in 1964 and 1965.

Financial assistance to the UNDP programs have also been substantial, considering India's economic status.

---

[77] *The United Nations Development Programme: India 1967*, New Delhi: United Nations Development Programme, 1967, pp. 14-15.

[78] *Ibid.*

Cash contributions to the Technical Assistance program increased from $250,000 in 1951 to $850,000 in 1965. As of 1965, she had contributed $12,505,000 to the Special Fund program. Annual total contributions to UNDP were $13,000,000 in 1966 and 1967.[79]

India's personnel contributions to peace-keeping efforts have been mentioned previously; further contributions in that sector have been made in terms of financial assistance. Between 1957 and 1962 India was assessed and paid a total of $2,101,367 for UNEF operations. India also contributes a substantial sum to the Asian Development Bank. As of 31 December, 1966, she had contributed $9,315,162, making her the third largest contributor.

---

[79] *Ibid.*

8

The Indian Public and
The United Nations

The Indian people have generally accepted, or at least not opposed, the broad outlines of Indian foreign policy, including membership and participation in the UN System. The small articulate segment concerned with foreign affairs has actively supported India's general participation in international organizations, though it has been critical of some Government positions on particular issues.

To what extent this broad consensus reflects the responsiveness of the Government to "public opinion," or whether on the contrary it is a result of the tendency of the public to accept and support, within broad limits, almost any foreign policy initiated by the Government, is uncertain, However, the latter seems to be a pronounced tendency even in such countries as the United States and the United Kingdom, where the level of literarcy is comparatively higher and voluntary groups make a greater effort to influence foreign policy than they do in India. the policies of the Government and the approach of its If one adds to these factors the dominance of the Congress

Party prior to 1967, it appears highly probable that Indian public opinion, or acceptance in the absence of opinion, has usually been more a reflection than a cause of foreign policy decisions. There is certainly little or no evidence to invalidate this generalization as far as the United Nations is concerned.

The considerable degree of Government latitude in foreign policy afforded by public opinion is reinforced by official attitudes. In academic circles it is generally believed that the Government is somewhat allergic to the presence and advice of non-official consultative bodies and that the attitude of officials is one of calculated indifference. In any case, there is a minimum of two-way flow of ideas between the Indian intellectual community and the Ministry of External Affairs as well as other Ministries involved in the administration of Indian foreign policy.

Yet on specific issues involving matters deemed important or vital to India, private groups and political parties do endeavour to exert influence. On these there is wide-spread comment in certain newspapers in the form of editorials, occasional articles, and letters to the editor. Political parties and other groups also make their views known either through the media of mass communication or through meetings, demonstrations, and various forms of public protest. Criticism of government policy has been particularly pronounced on the Hungarian, Tibetan, and West Asian problems. It is difficult to assess whether public dissatisfaction over the Government's hesitation to condemn Soviet intervention in Hungary when the issue was before the Security Council influenced the Government's later posture, although there is a widespread opinion that it did. On the Kashmir issue, the basic policies of the Government have not been seriously questioned, although there have been voices demanding the withdrawal of the dispute from the UN. In the West Asian crisis of 1967, the policies of the Government and the approach of its representative in the UN came under heavy fire both in the Parliament and in the press, as a result of which the Government was more or less on the defensive. Although the public has exercised very little influence on India's UN policies, with the weakening of the hold of the Congress Party on the country after 1967 the Government has become somewhat more responsive to public opinion on foreign policy issues.

This should not be taken to mean that the Government is not concerned with education of the public about the UN. In fact, it is active in this respect, and in doing so it does not arouse protests from "patriotic" groups as in the United States, where some of these view the UN as "subversive." The Indian National Commission for Cooperation with UNESCO, an agency of the Ministry of Education, has been the principal organ concerned with this program. The Indian field office of the United Nations Information Service (UNIS) works closely with the National Commission, as well as with other agencies at the Centre and in the states, in assisting the UN program in schools and informing the general public.

The National Commission, in cooperation with the Directorate of Advertising and Visual Publicity of the Ministry of Information and Broadcasting, issues material and broadcasts programs in celebration of United Nations Day, the Declaration of Human Rights, International Cooperation Year, etc. At the secondary school level, the Commission has encouraged the introduction of UN material in textbooks, distributed general information, and held teacher workshops in schools and in teacher

---

[80] Indian National Commission for UNESCO: *Secretary General's Report 1964-65,* New Delhi: Ministry of Education 1965, Also, *Report of the National Seminar on International Understanding* (New Delhi: Indian National Commission for UNESCO, 1956).

tra_ning institutes. It also maintains liaison with Departments of Public Instruction in the various states.[80]

The All-India Council for Secondary Education, composed of representatives of state governments and eminent
educators, is also concerned with teaching about the UN.
The United Schools Organization, an affiliate of the
United Schools International, maintains a Voluntary
Educational Centre for the United Nations in New Delhi,
and distributes material to students throughout India. It
conducts an annual All-India UN Test and distributes
prizes to the top ten contestants. Between 1958 and 1966,
92,273 students from 2,225 schools entered the contest.[81]

The Government is also involved in furthering knowl-
edge of the UN at the college and university level.
UNESCO Centres have been set up at a number of institutions, and at many others there is a UNESCO Corner
in the library where materials are available. In 1962, the
Vice-Chancellors and in the following year the Inter-
University Board, the latter at the behest of the National
Commission, approved a program for University collabo-
ration with UNESCO, especially in furtherance of its
East-West Project.[82] One of the results has been the establishment of permanent committees to carry out the program. For example, since 1963 Delhi University has had
a Committee for Continuous Cooperation to work with
the National Commission.

Several ministries in addition to Education either directly or indirectly help to publicize specific fields of UN
activity, or to highlight the Indian position on a specific
matter. The Ministry of Information and Broadcasting,
for example, has published factual material on issues in
which India is interested and has also published in book
form the important speeches of the Indian representatives
on issues such as Kashmir and Goa. At other times, the

---

[81] *World Informo* (New Delhi), March 1967.
[82] *New Letter* (New Delhi: INCU), March 1963, pp. 15-16.

various ministries have issued publications in conjunction with UNIS. Ministries concerned with health, tourism, food, agriculture and commerce all do so. Some important officials of the various ministries have also addressed meetings in order to explain the difficulties which they face at international conferences in furtherance of foreign policy goals. For example, the Indian representatives to the world conferences on the Law of the Sea, Law of Outer Space, and Disarmament, have tried to enlighten the people regarding the behind-the-scene diplomacy in order that they may have a realistic picture of the Government's position.

In addition to government bodies and universities, a number of institutions attempt to promote interest in and knowledge of the UN. The India International Centre, New Delhi, established in 1959, is recognized as an Associated Institution of UNESCO for South Asia to implement its Major Project II for Mutual Appreciation of Eastern and Western Cultures. The Indian Council of World Affairs, the Indian Society of International Law, the International Law Association (Indian Branch), and the Indian Federation of United Nations Associations are also involved in this educational effort. The All-India Women's Conference and the Indian Council of World Affairs are recognized as Category B non-governmental organizations associated with ECOSOC.[83]

Indian mass media also plays a role in educating the public and focusing attention on the UN, especially on specific matters considered by its various organs. However, as in other countries, the major newspapers do not provide systematic coverage, and the regional ones devote very little space to the system in general or to specific issues before it. Moreover, coverage is primarily concerned with problems of direct interest to India. The

---

[83] *Yearbook of the United Nations,* 1963, p. 395.

decisions of the UN on Kashmir, apartheid policies of the Union of South Africa and UN decisions and resolutions relating thereto, colonialism, disarmament, social welfare activities and similar problems are reported in the major press. The role played by the Secretary General, especially if he is a fellow Asian, has been prominently reported. When a UN agency holds meetings in New Delhi, the newspapers devoted special supplements to its organization and work in general. For example, in 1956 special supplements were issued by the major newspapers on the occasion of the 10th annual meeting of UNESCO in New Delhi, as they were for the UNCTAD Conference of 1968.

The educational role of radio in UN matters is limited. Only rarely do commentaries on UN activities constitute a part of radio programs. The weekly news round-up from the UN Radio in New York, however, is relayed from a few stations of All-India Radio. Occasionally a high UN dignitary visiting India is featured on a radio or television interview.

Despite the limitations, the record of India's effort to educate the public concerning the UN probably compares favorably with that of most other countries.

9

Summary

When India attained her long-sought goal of independence on August 15, 1947, she had for twenty-eight years been a member of the League of Nations and then of the UN. Only after September, 1946, however, when the Indian Interim Government was formed and British control in effect relinquished, were Indians able to make their own decisions *vis a vis* the world organization of which India was a member. Henceforth India was among the most active of the participants, both as a contributor to and as a beneficiary of the UN System.

One of the many tasks of the Indian Government was to prepare for this participation. Although a few Indians who had gained experience in the League or in the UN continued to serve the Government of an independent India in the UN System, for the most part those who did so were either newly recruited or reassigned and thus inexperienced in their new tasks. Likewise, whereas the new Government built upon the administrative structure of its predecessor, there was very little organization in existence for carrying out its responsibilities with respect to the UN System. Thus organization, as well as staffing for international organization purposes, have been, with minor exceptions, developments of the post-independence years.

The kind of organization and staff developed by the Indian Government to carry out its international organization tasks has been shaped in part by the kind of role that India has attempted to play in the UN System and the role of the UN within India. Both have been extensive.

India has continuously been an active participant in all the principal UN organs, all the Specialized Agencies, and in many of the subsidiary bodies of both. Individual Indians have served at all but the highest levels in the UN Secretariat, occupied the highest positions in some of the Specialized Agencies, and been called upon by the Secretary-General to aid in important peace-keeping activities. In terms of numbers of personnel India has ranked first in contributions to peace-keeping forces in both West Asia and the Congo. Despite her own need India has also been a major contributor to the UN System Technical Assistance Program. She has supplied over 2000 experts under the UNDP, and has provided training in India for several thousand persons from other developing countries. She ranks tenth in her contributions to the UN Regular Budget, and also makes important monetary contributions to the programs of the Specialized Agencies.

India clearly ranks first among the UN members as a beneficiary of its social and economic programs. In this respect she receives more than she gives. Indeed it would be strange were this not the case, given her population, needs, and capacity to take advantage of these contributions. The extensive Indian operations and contributions of the UNDP, several other UN organs, and the Specialized Agencies, especially WHO, FAO, UNESCO and the World Bank, are indicative of the extent of the supporting role of the UN System in Indian development.

There has been almost no expression of opposition to India's membership in the UN System, and on most particular issues the Government position has received wide support. Only on a few matters, especially those involving Tibet, West Asia, and Hungary, has the Government been severely criticized within India, and at least put on the defensive. On the whole, public opinion has been moulded by more than it has moulded India's UN policy.

The Government has both encouraged and undertaken extensive programs among the general public and in the schools to promote understanding of and support for the UN and its related agencies. The Indian National Commission for Cooperation with UNESCO, in effect an agency of the Ministry of Education, has been especially active in this regard. Other ministries of the Central Government, such as External Affairs and Information and Broadcasting, either on their own or in cooperation with the National Commission, have attempted to inform the Indian public about or to gain their support for the UN, especially on issues of particular concern to India.

Under the Indian federal and parliamentary system the Central Government, and within it the Cabinet, is endowed with ample legal authority to formulate and execute Indian policy in international organizations. The political situation has so far been conducive both to centralization of control and to its concentration within the Government. Although foreign policy, including India's position on UN System issues, has been subject to debate and criticism in both houses of Parliament, the Government has always been able to have its way on these matters.

The general organization of the Union Government, including its administrative structure, closely resembles that of the United Kingdom. Probably the greatest difference between the Indian (and United Kingdom) administration on the one hand and the United States administration on the other, lies in the more important role played by "officials," i.e., the permanent bureaucracy, in the former. In all three of these states, as well as in others, whereas one department or ministry is entrusted with certain primary foreign affairs tasks, most organs of government are concerned with both foreign and domestic policy and administration in the areas of their principal concern.

In India, as elsewhere, coordination, therefore, is "one of the major problems of the modern Civil Servant." The Indian system employs all the usual formal and informal coordinating devices found elsewhere. Nevertheless, there are differences between Washington, London, and New Delhi in this respect. There are considerably fewer formally institutionalized means, and especially fewer committees, at the lower levels in the Indian administrative hierarchy than in the other two countries. Whereas it is possible that through informal means and the circulation of files there is as much lower-level coordination in India as elsewhere, one gains the impression that this is not the case, and that either coordination of Indian foreign policy receives less attention than in the American or British system, or that most of it takes place at higher levels.

There are formal inter-organizational coordinating devices at various levels. Of these the cabinet is the highest, and within it the various cabinet committees, including that for External Affairs. At the next level there are committees of Secretaries, of which two-External Affairs and Economics—are especially concerned with foreign policy and UN policy as a part thereof. The Cabinet and its committees, as well as the Committees of Secretaries, are all served by the Cabinet Secretariat, headed by the Cabinet Secretary, the top-ranking permanent official. The Cabinet Secretary is chairman of the several Committees of Secretaries. The Cabinet Secretariat is also responsible for "follow-up" to see that decisions made in the committee are implemented. At a lower, but still relatively high level, the Policy Planning and Review Committee, a kind of Indian National Security Council, established in 1966, may become significant for the administration of Indian foreign policy toward the UN. Despite the existence of these and other committees, both intra-and inter-ministerial, the Indian Foreign Service Committee Report of 1966 indicated that in its opinion additional machinery was needed to enable the Ministry of External Affairs to meet its coordinating responsibilities.

In the case of most of these bodies, UN matters and even foreign policy in general are only a part of their responsibility. The same situation prevails in the case of the ministries themselves. Only the Ministry of External Affairs "specializes" in foreign policy, and its administration of UN matters is only a part of its general responsibility. Only at the lower organizational levels does one find specialists in UN matters. The UN and Conference and Disarmament Division of the External Affairs Ministry is the prime example, having developed in its present form only 1960. Just as the Ministry of External Affairs as a whole specializes in but does not monopolize the foreign affairs tasks, and has a major responsibility for inter-ministerial coordination, so does the UN Division share with other organs of the Ministry tasks regarding the UN and is entrusted with responsibility for intra-ministerial coordination.

At the highest levels, ministries other than External Affairs deal with foreign policy and UN matters as a part of their general responsibilities for national problems re-

gardless of their implications for foreign or domestic policy. At the same time most of them have found it necessary
to establish units whose primary or sole tasks are foreign
policy, or even the international organizational aspects of
that policy. Certainly that is true of the six ministries,
other than External Affairs, singled out for special consideration in this work. Thus in the Ministry of Finance
we find the External Finance and Foreign Aid Division
of the Department of Economic Affairs entrusted with
the Ministry's primary UN tasks. Within it are sections
and units especially concerned with the World Bank family of institutions. In the Ministry of Commerce the
General Commercial Wing, with its five subdivisions, is
responsible for India's relations with GATT, UNCTAD,
and ECAFE. UNESCO is the concern of the two units of
the UNESCO Division of the Ministry of Education. In
the Ministry of Food and Agriculture, most UN System
activities have been handled by the Foreign Aid Division
of the Department of Agriculture. The Labour Conference Section and Research Division of the Ministry of
Labour Employment and Rehabilitation is the primary
organ for handling India's relations with the ILO. Matters
involving WHO are dealt with by the International
Health Relations Division of the Department of Health
of the Ministry of Health and Family Planning. In the
Department of Family Planning, established in 1966, the
Secretariat wing coordinates work between central and
state agencies involved in family planning on the one
hand and the Specialized Agencies on the other. Although
details vary from ministry to ministry, there is a common
pattern of specialization on UN matters at the lower
organization levels in all.

India's UN tasks of course require that she be represented abroad, more or less continuously in New York,
Geneva, Washington, and Rome, and on numerous special occasions in these cities as well as elsewhere. Only in

New York and a few other places does India have full-time representatives specializing in UN work; for the most part this work is entrusted to members of the regular embassies or consultants on a part-time basis. In most of these special meetings, although the Ministry of External Affairs may be represented, the leadership and bulk of the membership of the Indian delegations are supplied by other Union Ministries, and sometimes by the states, or by appointment from among private parties.

Over the course of the years since 1947, as India has been concerned with UN affairs and as the UN has in turn become involved in India's problems, personnel and organization have evolved to enable the Indian Government to develop policies and implement programs related to the UN System. Although the organization structure will undoubtedly continue to develop and change, it is unlikely that there will be radical departures from the patterns which had evolved when these lines were written in 1968. When one compares the Indian arrangements for working with and through the UN system with those of other countries treated in this series, he is struck by the basic similarities rather than by the differences among them.

List of Abbreviations

ECAFE	—	Economic Commission for Asia and the Far East
ECE	—	Economic Commission for Europe
ECOSOC	—	Economic and Social Council
FAO	—	Food and Agricultural Organization
FAIT	—	Foreign Aid International Technical
FFHC	—	Freedom from Hunger Campaign
GATT	—	General Agreement on Tariffs and Trade
IAS	—	Indian Administration Service
IFS	—	Indian Foreign Service
ISI	—	Information Service of India
IBRD	—	International Bank for Reconstruction and Development
ICAO	—	International Civil Aviation Organization
IDA	—	International Development Association
IFC	—	International Finance Corporation
ILO	—	International Labour Organization
IMF	—	International Monetary Fund
INC	—	International Commission Unit
ITU	—	International Telecommunication Union
NCERT	—	National Council for Educational Research and Training
ONUC	—	United Nations Operations in the Congo
SF	—	Special Fund (UNDP)
TA	—	Technical Assistance (UNDP)
TAB	—	Technical Assistance Board
UGC	—	University Grants Commission
UN	—	United Nations
UNCTAD	—	United Nations Conference on Trade and Development
UNDP	—	United Nations Development Program
UNEF	—	United Nations Emergency Force
UNESCO	—	United Nations Educational Scientific and Cultural Organization
UNICEF	—	United Nations Children's Fund
UNIS	—	United Nations Information Service
UNMOGIP	—	United Nations Military Observation Group in India and Pakistan
USAID	—	United States Agency for International Development
WFP	—	World Food Program
WHO	—	World Health Organization
WMO	—	World Meteorological Organization
SCAPE	—	Special Committee for Assistance to African People

Index